Edinburgh and
the Eastern Lowlands

DISCOVERING BRITAIN

Edinburgh and the Eastern Lowlands

Lothian, Fife and the Borders

by

IONA McGREGOR

FABER AND FABER · London and Boston

First published in 1979
by Faber and Faber Limited
3 Queen Square London WC1
Filmset and printed in Great Britain by
BAS Printers Limited, Over Wallop, Hampshire

© *Iona McGregor, 1979*

British Library Cataloguing in Publication Data

McGregor, Iona
   Edinburgh and the Eastern Lowlands
   —(Discovering Britain).
   1. Scotland—Description and travel
   —Juvenile literature
   I. Title   II. Series
   914.13'04'857   DA867

   ISBN 0-571-11100-9

Contents

Illustrations

Acknowledgements

Faber and Faber wish to thank the following for permission to reproduce the photographs:
British Tourist Authority, Plates Nos. 1, 4, 5, 6, 12, 13, 14, 15; Hopetoun House Preservation Trust, Plate No. 17; The National Portrait Gallery, London, Plate No. 11; Scotsman Publications Ltd., Plate No. 9; Scottish Tourist Board, Plates Nos. 2, 3, 7, 8, 10, 16, 18, 19.

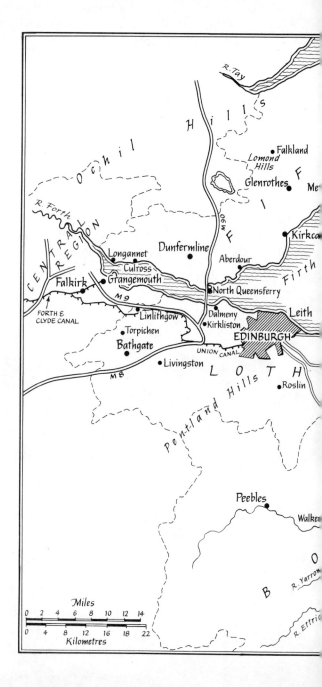

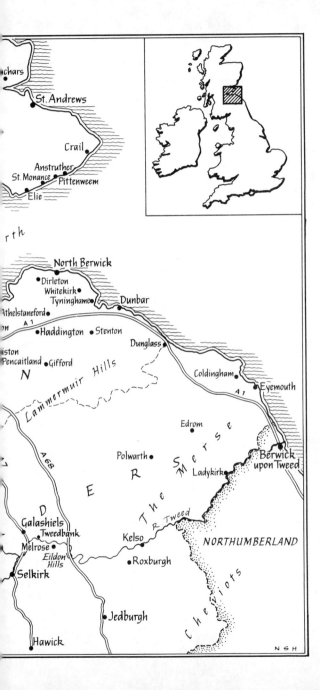

1 · The Land

Most people who do not know Scotland well think that it is divided into 'Highlands' and 'Lowlands', and assume that the Lowlands must be rather flat compared with the mountainous north. In fact, much of the Lowlands is very hilly, with vast stretches of grass and heather moor sweeping up to summits that are two thousand feet or more in height.

South of the Highland Line which runs from Stonehaven in the east to Greenock in the west Scotland consists of two parallel belts of land. Each of these is roughly fifty miles in depth, and they are known as the Midland Valley and the Southern Uplands. They run like two diagonal stripes from coast to coast separated by a feature known to geologists as the Southern Upland Fault. If you look at a map you will see that the hill-ranges in both these 'Lowland' areas follow the same south-west to north-east line as the areas themselves.

Intensive agriculture is impossible in Scotland anywhere above one thousand feet. In the hillier areas, even with modern transport and housing, life can become very harsh in winter. Towns have sprung up in more sheltered sites, but until recently, eastern Scotland has not been drawn into any major industrial activity. The pattern has not changed much since the late Middle Ages: a largely agricultural landscape is dotted with a vast number of small towns which either cling to the long coastline or serve as inland market-centres – Edinburgh, the capital and administrative heart of Scotland, dominating all. The total population of eastern Scotland has grown enormously in the last five hundred years, but it is distributed in the same way.

In 1973 the old counties were abolished and Scotland was divided into nine new regions. One of these is called the Borders and it takes in the four counties that were originally administered from the four ancient towns of Berwick, Roxburgh, Selkirk and Peebles. So the new region covers more or less the same area as what is traditionally known as 'the Border' between Scotland and England.

The River Tweed flows a hundred miles, west to east, through the Borders; with its northern and southern tributaries it cuts through the hills in long, deep dales that are still the main routes across the central Border. The Tweed begins at Tweed's Well in Peeblesshire. On the other side of the watershed is the source of the River Clyde. The Tweed comes down through bare, grassy hills that stretch in whale-backed summits into Ettrick Forest. Among them is St. Mary's Loch, which so delighted Wordsworth when he visited it in 1814, and the waters of Ettrick and Yarrow, which join the Tweed further east. With the Cheviots, these hills form the largest sheep-rearing area in Britain.

The first hunters and fishers probably came to Scotland in about 5000 B.C. They penetrated far up these valleys, which at that time were heavily wooded with oak, ash, alder, birch, pine, and other trees. From then until the mid-eighteenth century the forests were gradually reduced, and the soil became less and less fertile. The wood was needed for fuel and building, and later for iron smelting. Some of the ground was deliberately cleared for growing crops; but most of the damage was probably done by goats and sheep and other animals. They nibbled away the young saplings that would have replaced the old growth. It is likely that the Iron Age Celts used the lower hill-slopes for grazing their flocks, and that the more thickly-wooded valleys were not cleared until

1. St. Mary's Loch, set among the green hills of Ettrick Forest, is a famous beauty-spot in the Borders

the Angles came in the sixth century A.D. The Celts seem to have grown some grain near their homesteads, but they were mostly pastoral people. They probably began the shieling system that lasted until the eighteenth century: that is, in summer the sheep, goats and cattle were taken to upland pastures. There they soon cleared the forest glades and left bare hill-sides that now produce only deer-grass, heather, bog-mosses and bracken.

The extinction of the forests went on all over southern Scotland. It was held back slightly by laws to preserve the woods as hunting-grounds for monarchs and nobility. Robert the Bruce hunted in the Pentland Forest.

The Border forests probably disappeared faster than the rest. Sheep-rearing has been an industry there since the Cistercian and Benedictine monks introduced it in the twelfth century. The Border abbeys were built largely from the profit on the wool-crop, which was exported through the then Scottish port of Berwick-on-Tweed. In 1530 James V led a twelve-thousand-strong hunting expedition to Ettrick Forest – his real purpose was to flush out the outlaws hiding there. He destroyed much of the Forest and then pastured ten thousand sheep on the land. Another great surge of deforestation probably took place after the Union of the Crowns in 1603. On 24 March 1603 Queen Elizabeth I died, and the King of Scots, James VI, became James I of England as well. For the first time in three hundred years there was peace in the Borders. Even larger flocks were grazed on the hills, and today's huge sheep-walks came into being.

The bare Border hills are patched with green and russet bracken, and in June there is a blaze of yellow gorse near the stony valley floors. The heather comes into bloom in late autumn. All this beautiful vegetation is however proof of how poor the soil now is, compared with its state hundreds of years ago. The Forestry Commission and private landowners are trying to bring back the woodland. The soil is now so thin that often it will take only monotonous wedges of dark spruce or the slightly lighter Lodgepole pine; but mixed planting is tried wherever possible.

The new forests are even invading some of the old sheep-walks, and there is an encouraging return of wild life to these wide-open spaces. The curlew and peewit and birds of prey have always been found in the upland moors; now wild goats and roe deer are becoming more plentiful, and there are more badgers and red squirrels in the new woods.

In the middle of its hundred-mile journey the Tweed becomes a broad smooth river. Beyond Peebles and Innerleithen it is at its most beautiful, with great loops and meanders that flow past lush wooded pastures and large country houses, including the best known of all – Abbotsford,

2. Scott's view over the triple-peaked Eildon Hills and the River Tweed. The horses drawing his funeral carriage stopped here, as they had always done when their master was alive

once the home of Sir Walter Scott. Because his home was here, and he wrote so much about it, this area is known as 'the Scott country'. Here are the famous Border abbeys, and a group of attractive country towns that we shall look at more closely in the next chapter. They are all ancient settlements, and sprang up on the routeways of the Tweed and its tributaries. They survived constant attack from English invaders from the thirteenth to sixteenth centuries.

Ice movement during the Glacial Age scraped the Border hills into their rounded shapes, and deposited boulder clay along the river valleys. The melting glaciers later dumped more sand and gravel. As a result the middle Tweed valley is a prosperous farming area of large, square fields bounded by hedges, copses, shelter-belts and game-coverts. The landscape is made more attractive by the not-so-distant hills. From nearly every view you can see the triple volcanic peaks of the Eildons, which gave the name of 'Trimontium' to the Roman camp at their base. It was by this route that Agricola, the Roman governor of Britain, drove his main road into Scotland in A.D. 80.

At Kelso the Tweed meets its last main Scottish tributary, the Teviot. Then the valley broadens out into what is known on the Scottish side as the Merse. This is the largest plain in Scotland. Here there are large arable farms producing barley, potatoes, oats and turnips. On the east side of the Merse the Tweed becomes for about fifteen miles the border between Scotland and England. Looking at this area today it is hard to believe it was once part of the most fought-over region in the British Isles.

After the Romans withdrew, England was invaded by the Angles and Saxons, and south-eastern Scotland eventually became part of the Anglian kingdom of Northumbria. This stretched from the Humber to the Forth. However, Viking raids weakened and separated the northern Angles from those in the south, and the part north of the Tweed fell to the King of Scots in 1018.

When the Normans arrived, with their complicated system of vassalage and land-ownership, confusion returned. The Scottish royal house intermarried with both Normans and the deposed Anglo-Saxon family. There were invasions from both sides, with Scotland and England each claiming and seizing part of the other's kingdom.

The Border line was finally fixed in 1237 by the Treaty of York. It was an artificial boundary, most of it skimming the Cheviots, the smooth, grassy-backed hills that form the southern rim of the Tweed basin. But the treaty did not bring peace. Fifty years later began the quarrel between various Norman-Scots about who should inherit the Scottish crown. Edward I, 'Hammer of the Scots', claimed that he was their overlord, and so rightful King of Scots.

This led to various English invasions, and the counter-attacks of Wallace and Bruce. Time and time again terrible disasters befell the people of the Borders. Jedburgh, Rox-burgh, and even Edinburgh Castles were destroyed by the Scots themselves to prevent English occupation. Berwick-on-Tweed changed hands fourteen times before it finally became an English town in 1482. In the mid-sixteenth century Henry VIII sent his army twice into Scotland, and they devastated the country as far north as Edinburgh. This was because he was trying to break the alliance between Scotland and France, and wanted the young Mary Queen of Scots to marry his own heir.

During these three hundred years of strife officials called Wardens of the Marches were appointed by Scots and English to settle Border disputes. Not surprisingly, they found it as difficult to control their own followers as to fend off enemy invasion. The Humes, the Scotts, the Douglases, the Kerrs, the Armstrongs, and many others, had little respect for the great landowners who were supposed to control them. They were known as moss-troopers, or reivers. Jock o' the Side, Kinmont Willie, and Johnnie Armstrong have left their names enshrined in the immortal Border Ballads, along with their thefts of sheep and cattle, which have been turned into heroic adventures.

They have also left their mark on the buildings of the region. Very few survive from the early period except abbeys, churches, and the fortified houses known as peel-towers. There are a vast number of these, mostly along the Tweed and its tributaries, where the raids were likely to come.

The northern rim of the Tweed basin is Lammermuir and the Lammermuir Hills. This is a bleaker, flatter tableland than the Cheviots. It too was once thickly wooded, but now is almost treeless. Beyond Lammermuir is the Lothian plain.

You can enter the Lothians by two routes, both of which bring you over Lammermuir. You can follow the Great North Road, the A1, through Cockburnspath and Dunbar. You will be passing some of the finest coastal scenery in Britain, but you will not see much of it unless you make a special detour. The coastline is deeply indented, and the road often swings inland. Or you can follow the A68, Agricola's road, up Lauderdale. These are both ancient routes. The A7, which runs beside the Gala Water, four miles west of the A68, is a comparative youngster. It was not usable in winter until the early nineteenth century. The A68 climbs to the top of the Lammermuirs up a long rise called Soutra. From the top there is a marvellous view. Beyond the red fields of East Lothian you can see the broadening waters of the Firth of Forth, with more hills beyond, and to your left the Pentland Hills and the romantic skyline of Edinburgh.

Like the Merse, East Lothian is a rich agricultural area. The red sandstone which is used in many of the older buildings has weathered down to give the soil its well-known chocolate colour. If you come in autumn you will see the acres of golden grain that amazed the soldiers of Oliver Cromwell when they invaded Scotland in 1650. Robert Burns came here in 1787 and called it 'the most glorious corn country that I ever saw'.

The new region of Lothian is made up of the three former counties of East, Mid and West Lothian. The last two merge into Scotland's industrial belt, which stretches across the narrow isthmus between the Forth and the Clyde, and spreads into adjacent areas. About eighty per cent of Scotland's population (five and a quarter million) live in this central area. There is now a much denser population towards the west, in the Strathclyde region, but until the Industrial Revolution, the part round the Forth basin was the most thickly populated in Scotland.

This was partly because government and law were centred in Edinburgh, as they still are, and partly because early Scots trade looked eastwards to the Low Countries and the Baltic.

There are about two dozen harbours on the north and south shores of the Forth, which is tidal up to Stirling. They were once used not only for fishing, but also for trade across the North Sea. They were all fairly shallow tidal harbours; at low tide the ships were left keeled over in the mud. This did not matter until the nineteenth century, when ships became far larger. When engineers tried to deepen the harbours, they came across the Forth's buried river-channel that had been cut during the Ice Age. Later this was filled in by silt and mud, and the small towns that owned the harbours could not afford to clean it. So overseas trade became concentrated in a few larger harbours, such as Kirkcaldy, Leith and Grangemouth. Other ports became holiday centres, or fishing villages.

The eastern Forth harbours survived for trading longer than many others because their chief traffic was in coal from the Fife and Lothian coal-fields. Until the development of railways it was easiest to carry coal by sea, even to neighbouring towns. There was a sea-borne coal trade from the eastern Forth ports from the early Middle Ages. This went on into the era when Britain exported large amounts of coal overseas. In 1913, Methil in south Fife exported two and a half million tons of coal a year.

In all parts of Britain coal-mining is now a shrinking industry, and is concentrated in a few intensively-worked pits. So whereas East Lothian is agricultural, with a few charming small towns and villages, and Midlothian is overrun by the suburban development of Edinburgh, West Lothian, where a lot of the disused pits are, seems to the visitor to be full of derelict buildings and unused colliery machinery. Dotted round about here are also the red mounds left by the old shale-mining industry, which has now vanished. So anyone passing through on the main roads takes away the impression that West Lothian is not an attractive area. This is unfortunate, for hidden away it has some pleasant hill country and several important monuments: these include a royal palace at Linlithgow, Cairnpapple Hill which is the finest prehistoric site in south-eastern Scotland, and some of its best mediaeval church architecture.

North of the Forth estuary is the Kingdom of Fife, as it still calls itself. When local government was being reorganized in 1973 Fife put up a determined fight not to be divided between the two giant regions to north and south, and eventually won. This incident is very typical of the Fifers, as its people are called, for they have always been very proud of being a separate and self-contained region of Scotland.

Lying between the Firths of Forth and Tay, Fife juts into the North Sea, like a tuning-fork with two hill-ranges forming the prongs. These flatten out as they get near the sea. On the north side are the Ochil Hills running in from Strathallan, and on the south the two Lomond Hills, the Cleish Hills, and other small, broken summits. In between the two ranges is the Howe ('hollow') of Fife, a farming area like East Lothian. Most of inland Fife is agricultural, and the countryside is quiet and pleasant.

However, for its size, Fife is probably the most interesting region in Scotland. It has sixteen ancient and historic towns, most of which line the sixty miles of Fife's southern coastline. Many of them are now just charming little villages; but they were once important trading-ports. After the Romans withdrew, Fife became one of the seven Kingdoms of the Picts. They held most of north-eastern Scotland until they were conquered by Kenneth MacAlpin, King of Scots, about A.D. 850. Later, Dunfermline with its abbey and palace was the home and capital of the Norman kings and queens of

Scotland. Fife's most famous city, St. Andrews, was the religious capital of the whole country, and in 1411 the first Scottish university was founded there. It is also of course a famous golfing city.

It was not until the eighteenth century that Fife became a prosperous agricultural area. Until then, the central part was full of lakes and swamps. Most of these have now been drained. The eastern part has many small streams that run through rock gorges or 'dens', sometimes as deep as one hundred feet. Dura Den is world-famous for the fossils that were discovered in its rocks. Although grain is now grown right up to the edge of the cliffs, much of the coastline, as in Lothian and Berwickshire, is low grassy ground that makes splendid links, or golf-courses.

South-west Fife contains the Fife coal-field. This also runs under the bed of the Forth, sealed in by the boulder-clay on the river-bed. Coal has been worked in Fife for over a thousand years. It appears near the surface in many places, so open-cast mining has been common. The whole area is pitted and humped from ground subsidence and overgrown mine-workings. But there have been efforts lately to repair the damage to the landscape. At Lochore Meadows there is the biggest reclamation scheme in Britain. Rows of empty cottages, unused winding-gear, and acres of flooded land are gradually being brought back from their derelict state and turned into a vast recreation area. Thirty years ago there were forty-two pits working in west central Fife. Today there are only five.

Next to Fife are the two small counties of Kinross and Clackmannan, now part of the new Central Region. Kinross is a scooped-out basin between the Lomond, Cleish and Ochil Hills. At its centre is Loch Leven, famous for angling, and also for the island castle where Mary Queen of Scots was imprisoned for a year. Clackmannan is the smallest Scottish county. It is saucer-shaped, and only eight miles across each way. It is like a saucer bent across the middle: it is almost exactly divided between flat ground bordering the River Forth, and the steep southern slope of the Ochil Hills, with several small towns perched at their foot.

2 · Towns and Villages

Most towns and villages in the Scottish Lowlands show clear traces of their mediaeval past. The older buildings usually keep more or less to the ancient street plan.

In southern England, country towns often grew up on the site of Roman army camps, or were laid out by Roman surveyors as tribal capitals to control the new province. In Scotland, however, the Roman occupation never got beyond the stage of military police-work. The first real towns, or *burghs,* appeared in the reign of David I, in the twelfth century.

David spent much of his early life in England, and he married the King of England's sister. He brought back to Scotland many Norman friends who helped him set up the feudal system there. David granted land to his vassals in return for certain duties, usually military. They in turn granted land to their own vassals, and so on. It was an excellent way of controlling parts of the country the King could not keep an eye on himself.

David divided the country into sheriffdoms. These later formed the counties which disappeared only in 1973. A sheriff managed each sheriffdom from a royal castle which usually controlled some important route or river crossing. The castles at Edinburgh and Stirling are good examples.

People settled round the castles, partly for protection, and partly to make a living by supplying the garrison with food, clothes, and other things. When the community grew large enough they began making laws for themselves and anyone who wished to join them. The householders were known as *burgesses* and there were strict rules about who could follow the various crafts and trades in their town, and how disputes should be settled among them. The King gave a charter which listed the rights and duties of these burgesses; and, very important from his point of view, what rents and taxes they had to pay him.

These towns were known as *royal burghs*, and David I erected about fifteen of them. Later rulers erected many more. Great lords and churchmen were allowed to erect burghs in other areas, and these were known as *burghs of barony*. Of course people had gathered together before; but that was more by chance. Each burgh was deliberately set up for a purpose; and they first appeared when overseas trade and organized exchange of goods began in Scotland. The first Scottish silver pennies were minted in the reign of David I (1124–1153).

Each burgh controlled an area in which all goods had to be brought to the burgh to be bought and sold. The royal burghs had more rights than the others over overseas trade; and more trade meant more money for the King. James VI remarked that David had been 'a sore saint for the crown' – meaning that he had given too much to the church, including the right to set up so many burghs. He himself raised many burghs of barony to royal status, and so took their rents for himself.

The typical Scottish burgh was most prosperous in the sixteenth and seventeenth centuries. It sent out coal, wool, hides and salted fish, and imported luxuries such as wine, spices, fine cloth, or materials in short supply – for instance timber and iron.

Most of Scotland's trade then was with France and the Low Countries, and the Baltic. So most of the burghs are found in eastern Scotland, and there is a thick cluster of them in Fife and the Lothians. The East Neuk of Fife has a delightful collection. At first glance they seem to be only pretty fishing

3. Crail, a picturesque fishing town in the East Neuk of Fife

villages. But if you walk round and use your eyes, you will see
that Crail, for instance, has a very wide main street; it was one
of the biggest market-places in mediaeval Europe. All these
'villages' had market-crosses and large tolbooths (town halls),
marking a status far beyond their present size.

Crail, Anstruther, Pittenweem, St. Monance and Elie all
have their individual character; but there is a family likeness
among them. They are built in local stone, usually a warm
brownish colour. There are stately merchant-houses in the
main street, and fisher-cottages with picturesque outside stairs
in the steep wynds leading down to the harbour. Sometimes

the walls are washed in brilliant white, or other colours. This is known as harling. The roofs are mostly covered with red pantiles, first brought from the Low Countries. There is quite a strong Dutch influence in the buildings. Some of the gables are hipped in the Dutch fashion; most of them however are 'crow-stepped', a fashion that lasted in Scotland until the end of the eighteenth century.

The National Trust for Scotland has carefully restored many little houses along the coast of Fife. In Culross, (pronounced *Cóo-russ*) further west, it has taken on a whole town. The central area is now restored to its original appearance, complete with bumpy rounded cobbles.

The town was at first a settlement attached to Culross Abbey; but as a seventeenth-century burgh it was created by Sir George Bruce, who developed the local industries of coal-mining, salt-panning, and iron-working. He made himself very rich by doing this. Culross was famous for its girdles, the flat baking-plates used to make scones. Bruce drove mine-galleries under the bed of the Forth and built himself a house in the town, rather grandly known as the Palace. You can look round it, and several other houses, and there is an excellent guide-book pointing out all the interesting features of the town. You will see some of the painted timber ceilings which are special to seventeenth-century Scotland.

The most famous town in Fife is St. Andrews, set in a magnificent bay that sweeps out on one side to jagged cliffs and the headland of Fife Ness, and on the other to a stretch of sand that ends at the River Eden. You can see the Angus hills across the Firth of Tay and, on a clear day, the Grampian foothills.

Despite its fine site St. Andrews did not become an important port, mainly because the bay has always been treacherous water. In one version its history begins with a shipwreck. Regulus, a monk of Patras in Greece, is supposed to have been cast up here with the bones of the apostle St. Andrew.

From about the eighth century A.D. St. Andrews became the religious centre of Scotland, and a place of pilgrimage. There was an early church, St. Mary's, of which the foundations still remain, and a tall, square tower, called St. Rule's, is supposed to have been part of the first priory.

The centre of the town still quite obviously follows the mediaeval street-line. The three main streets all run towards the cathedral, founded about 1160. As planned, it was the longest church in Britain, after Norwich Cathedral, and it must have been an impressive sight to homing ships on the top of the cliffs. It is now completely ruined except for the west towers and a few fragments of wall. Popular myth says it was wrecked during the Reformation. In fact, it was a difficult building to finish, and it was damaged several times by fire and storm. Neglect more than deliberate vandalism brought it to its present state. After the Reformation, it was robbed for building-stone. Many houses in the city have sections of its carved stones built into them.

The Priory buildings have almost disappeared too, except for the wall built round their grounds by Prior Hepburn in the mid-sixteenth century. This is the same date as the West Port, which is the only Scottish town gate surviving in its original form.

A few hundred yards from the Cathedral is the castle-palace of the Bishops and Archbishops of St. Andrews. Both English and Scots battered it, and a lot has slid into the sea. There is still much of it left, including a bottle-dungeon, and a unique mine and counter-mine left over from the siege of 1546–7. This followed the murder of Cardinal Beaton, when his assassins shut themselves into the Castle for a year. John Knox the Reformer was involved in this incident; you will find more details about the siege on page 78.

It would be wrong to give the idea that St. Andrews is a museum of ruined buildings. During most of the year it is a

4. The Castle of St. Andrews, closely associated with the violent events of the Scottish Reformation. Cardinal Beaton was murdered here in 1546

lively university town. The old colleges, founded from 1411 onwards, have been swamped by modern buildings on the edge of the town; but the students still wear the mediaeval scarlet gown, adding colour to the old grey streets. St. Andrews is also the home of golf, with four famous courses. The Royal and Ancient as it is simply known, the club-house overlooking the oldest course, is the final court of appeal for golfers and golfing disputes all over the world.

St. Andrews is a very popular holiday resort as well, and thousands of tourists come to it every year. In August it is visited by the Lammas Fair. This is the ancient street-market that has reached a final stage of dodgems, swings, shooting-stalls and fortune-telling. During the summer St. Andrews is probably the busiest town of its size in Scotland.

In the valley of the upper Tweed and its tributaries is a group of very ancient towns. On a map one can plainly see how they sprang up at river-crossings, or at meeting-points of routes through the Border hills.

Hawick on the River Teviot and Galashiels on the Gala Water are noted for their tweeds and knitwear. So is Selkirk, which stands a little below the meeting of the Yarrow and Ettrick Waters. It still has the old sheriff court-house where Sir Walter Scott – known locally as the 'Shirra' – presided for twenty-one years. His statue stands outside. There is another statue in the High Street of the explorer of Africa, Mungo Park, who was born nearby. Selkirk was formerly the capital town of Ettrick Forest, and has one of the oldest Common Ridings in the Borders. You will read more about that in Chapter Seven. Before becoming a woollen town Selkirk was famous for its souters or shoemakers. It provided two thousand pairs of shoes for Prince Charlie's army in 1745.

These three towns make good touring and angling centres. More attractive for its own sake is Kelso, standing where the Tweed and the Teviot meet. At first, it was only a small settlement, attached to Kelso Abbey, and overshadowed by its mighty neighbours, the royal burgh and castle of Roxburgh. But Roxburgh was repeatedly destroyed in the Border wars; after the mid-sixteenth century both castle and town faded away, and Kelso became important. It has a very attractive central cobbled square, and a graceful bridge built by John Rennie. He used the same plan later in old Waterloo Bridge, in London. When this was demolished, two of its iron lamps were placed on the Kelso bridge.

In Kelso David I founded the first of the four great Border abbeys. This was in 1126, for some monks he had brought from France. They had gone to Selkirk first, but stayed only ten years, as the site did not allow them to develop their farming activities. Kelso Abbey owned mills, fisheries, manors and farms throughout southern Scotland, and did much to improve agriculture in the area. But it suffered terribly in the Anglo-Scottish wars. On the last raid, in 1545, the English commander turned his guns directly on the Abbey tower and the defenders were massacred. Only part of the western tower remains, with arcaded transepts separated by tall, straddling arches. But it is impressive even as a ruin, dominating the centre of Kelso.

Monasteries and nunneries came very late to Scotland. The earlier clergy, who were more like the monks of the Celtic church, were known as Culdees. Queen Margaret, the wife of Malcolm Canmore (who comes into Shakespeare's *Macbeth*), began to change the rites of this older church; and her son, David I, divided Scotland into ten dioceses ruled by bishops. He also began founding abbeys, priories and nunneries. With the King's castles which controlled the sheriffdoms they helped to weld Scotland together.

Melrose is in the lushest part of the Tweed valley. It is a small, attractive town lying between the river and the triple-peaked Eildons. A few miles down the Tweed there had already been a monastery of Celtic monks. One of its first abbots was St. Cuthbert. David I brought Cistercian monks here from Rievaulx in Yorkshire. The Cistercians devoted themselves to prayer and labour; when the first site proved too bleak for farming, David settled them in 1136, at New

5. Melrose Abbey suffered badly during English raids across the Border. Fortunately much of its fine detailed stonework still survives

Melrose, the present site of the Abbey. Unfortunately, Melrose, like Kelso, was in the Middle March, very close to the ancient Roman route from Corbridge to the Lothians. So the Abbey was at the mercy of any raiding force from the south. It was attacked and destroyed several times.

The ruins seen today date from about 1400 – 1500. By then the simple building style used by the early Cistercians had changed into something far more elaborate. There is a lot of lavish decoration and tracery, and this makes Melrose the most interesting of the abbeys to look at in detail. Much of the stonework is a deep rose colour; the style is late Decorated and Perpendicular, as at York Minster. In days when books were scarce and few people could read, churches provided information that now we get from print or television. Bible stories and characters were used freely in the decoration. But not all the carvings are of sacred subjects. The church absorbed people's lives so completely that it had room for humour as well. Look out for the gargoyles and demons and hobgoblins that grimace on the buttresses and gables. There is a cook with his ladle, a comical pig playing the bagpipes, and dozens of grotesque heads. In other places the carvings burst into graceful leaves and buds and flowers.

6. Mary Queen of Scots House, Jedburgh. Besides having relics of the Queen in its small museum the house is a good example of late sixteenth-century Scottish architecture

The worst damage was inflicted on Melrose in 1545, the year of the 'Rough Wooing', as the Scots called it. This was their ironic name for Henry VIII's attempt to make them hand over the young Mary Queen of Scots as a bride for the Prince of Wales, the future Edward VI. This time there was no money or will to restore the Abbey. It was the eve of the Reformation. The whole idea behind the monastic way of life had been corrupted. Lay abbots or commendators had been appointed to many Scottish abbeys, and they were more interested in enjoying the rich revenues than in improving or repairing the buildings.

Jedburgh is another place that owes its fame to an abbey founded by King David. It stands even further south on the A68, and like the other towns of the Middle March was often attacked and destroyed. But at Jedburgh the abbey church is complete up to the wallhead, with a splendid nave and a fine rose window on the west front.

There are other interesting things to be seen in the town. The original castle was demolished in 1409 to stop it being used as a base by English raiders; the so-called 'Castle' is an early nineteenth-century jail. The most famous building after the Abbey is the house where Queen Mary lay ill in 1556 after riding to see the Earl of Bothwell at Hermitage Castle. There are several relics of the Queen in the house museum, including her death-mask. Just south of the town is a thousand-year-old oak, known as the Capon Tree, which is said to be the one tree surviving from the ancient Jed Forest.

The fourth Border abbey is Dryburgh. This lies five miles downstream from Melrose. There is very little of the abbey church left, but a lot of the cloisters and monks' living-quarters. Sir Walter Scott and Field-Marshal Earl Haig are buried here.

Apart from their historic buildings, the Borders towns are busy market and service centres for the farming communities surrounding them. They are all small: Hawick, the largest, has a population of roughly sixteen thousand. Peebles, Coldstream, Duns and Lauder are a few more that you might like to visit.

The Scottish burghs kept a tight hold of their trading monopolies until the late seventeenth century. In the south-east there were so many of them that rural communities hardly had the chance to develop. Villages in the English sense – a small settlement with its own church, inn, shop, smithy, and possibly manor-house, all clustering round a main street or village green – hardly existed in Scotland. The exception was usually found in the Merse and Lothians area settled by Anglians from the south. Stenton and Dirleton in East Lothian, and Ceres in Fife, are three rare and pretty examples of Scottish villages.

Even so, what we see today is not often directly connected with any mediaeval settlement. It is usually the work of the 'Improvers'. These were eighteenth-century landowners and farmers who brought the agricultural revolution to Scotland. You will read about them in detail in the next chapter. With the new methods of raising crops and livestock they also improved farm equipment and buildings. This meant that fewer people were needed actually to work on the land. So the Improvers built villages for them to live in. There they worked as traders or craftsmen – tailors, blacksmiths, weavers of linen and wool. They also provided a market for the farm produce. Sometimes of course the village was a housing scheme for workers on the landowner's estate.

Athelstaneford, Gifford and Tyninghame in East Lothian are villages founded or rebuilt in the eighteenth century. They and many others were all modelled on Ormiston, again in East Lothian. This was founded in 1738 by the local landowner John Cockburn to provide work for his tenants in brewing, milling, starch-making, market-gardening, mining, and other activities. Cockburn had to supervise the work from London, where he had a Government post, but he kept a strict eye on the way both his estate and the town developed. He wrote in 1742, 'I can give my consent to no houses being built in the Main Street of the Town but what are two Storys High . . . Good handsome houses sets off the place'. Ormiston still has its 'good handsome houses'. Sadly, when he was nearly seventy, after spending much energy on projects that later brought so much benefit to his country, John Cockburn fell into debt and had to sell his own estate to the Earl of Hopetoun.

The eighteenth century brought fine Georgian buildings not only to the country estates and new villages, but to the larger towns as well. Haddington, once the county town of East Lothian, grew up round its twelfth-century Abbey. The central area round the old market-place has been finely restored. It has some very attractive buildings in the classical style, including a town house by William Adam.

The railways had an enormous effect on Scottish towns. Many of the Fife and Lothian ports became holiday centres almost by accident; but before long the railway promoters realized that their iron roads could create new population centres, as well as exploit existing ones. This is what happened at North Berwick. Building development there was meant to turn a smallish grain port into a high-class commuters' suburb, linked to the offices of Edinburgh. Things did not quite turn out like that; but expansion came anyway, because the railway could now take golfers to the beautiful, windswept fairways of East Lothian.

The string of championship golf-courses at Gullane and Muirfield are the result of sand sweeping in from the Forth between 1590 and 1600. Farms were buried, and the parish church at last had to be abandoned. However, the disaster was turned into gain in the nineteenth century, when the railways opened up this area. For a time, the Lothian Coast Express brought fanatic golfers here from as far away as Glasgow for a day on the links, and then took them back the next morning.

The railway also turned North Berwick and Dunbar into lively centres for family holidays. Dunbar is full of old red sandstone buildings. The castle overlooking the sea was an important strong-point in the struggles between Scots and English, and was finally destroyed by order of the Scottish Parliament in 1567.

The old harbour was begun by Oliver Cromwell, who in 1650 defeated the Scottish Covenanters under General Leslie, a little way outside the town. In the later seventeenth century it gave work to twenty thousand people who helped salt the herring catch. It also sent out a whaling fleet in the eighteenth century. Now the only ships using the harbour are small inshore fishing-boats.

All the towns mentioned so far are built of local limestone and sandstone. The eastern Lowlands are well supplied with stone quarries. The roofs are red pantiles, or, more commonly, slates. These materials are now too expensive to use and modern housing developments look much like their counterparts in England.

The twentieth century has brought two completely new towns to south-eastern Scotland. They are Glenrothes in Fife and Livingston in West Lothian. Glenrothes was planned immediately after World War II (1939–45). It was hoped that the Fife coal industry would expand, and Glenrothes was built to house miners and their families. This did not happen, and Glenrothes is now a centre for light industry.

Livingston was begun twenty years later, for the overspill population of Glasgow. It too houses workers in light industry. Both these towns are quite different in their appearance and lay-out from the more traditional communities we have been looking at.

Partly through accident, and partly through planning, the industry of the Midland Valley has not been allowed to spoil the attractions of Scotland's capital city. The accident belongs to the geological factors that gave it its striking situation.

Overlooking the plain between the Pentland Hills and the sea, there is a high volcanic rock. In a sixth-century Welsh poem it was called 'Dineiden'. Celtic chieftains, Angles, Scots, Normans, and the invading English all fought to possess it. It was the main strong-point in the region. We can clearly see why, when we look up from Princes Street at the most famous landmark in Edinburgh, the Castle Rock.

Edinburgh's suburbs and industrial fringe stretch out about ten miles from east to west, and six from north to south. They are much like those of any other city. Visitors come for the few square miles in the centre. This contains other hills besides the Castle Rock, and for them, as well as the fame of its writers and scholars, Edinburgh was called 'the Athens of the North'.

Central Edinburgh is really two cities. The Old Town owes its spectacular skyline to the crag-and-tail formation of the Castle Rock. The hard volcanic core of the Rock acquired a 'tail' of debris as the Ice Age glaciers scraped over it. Down this tail straggled the burgh that looked to the royal castle for protection. Building was cramped by the steep sides of the ridge, and the sodden ground below it. So Edinburgh's houses rose to staggering heights down what became known as the Royal Mile; that is, the steep cobbled hill between the Castle and Holyrood Palace. The original timber and plaster buildings were at great risk from fire. So they were replaced by the stone tenements we see today. In between the buildings or under the first storey ran the wynds, or closes. One English traveller compared the High Street and its lanes to 'a double wooden comb, the great street the wood in the middle and the teeth of each side the lanes'. Originally in all Scottish burghs the houses were built with their gable-ends to the street and garden-plots behind. This ground was soon built over, and so the wynds were the means of access to inner courtyards, or rows of buildings behind the street-line.

People entered the houses, or 'lands' by spiral staircases ('turnpikes') opening on to the street or close. An amazing number of people packed into these early high-rise buildings. Daniel Defoe was up in Scotland to promote the 1707 Treaty of Union with England, and remarked, 'In no city in the world do so many people live in so little room'. He made many admiring comments about the beauty and strength of the grim old lands. Other travellers were not so pleased. They were scandalized by a notorious habit of Edinburgh householders, who threw out household refuse on to the pavement (and passers-by). This happened every night at ten p.m. with only the briefest warning, of 'Gardez-loo!' The stench from the rubbish and slops lasted until scavengers removed them at dawn. It was known as 'the Flowers o' Edinburgh'.

Everybody, of all social classes, lived in the lands. So this crowded mile produced a rich bag of 'characters'. Many of them are immortalised in John Kay's *Edinburgh Portraits*. Kay was a late-eighteenth-century barber who produced engravings of well-known Edinburgh people. Later they were collected and re-published with stories and anecdotes, and they form the best social history of their times.

By then Edinburgh's second city was being built – the New Town, as it is confusingly called, although its buildings are now one hundred to two hundred years old. The term is applied to the square mile north of Princes Street, all of which is now a conservation area. The crescents, squares, circuses and terraced streets of the New Town are the most important example of Georgian town-planning in existence. Princes Street and George Street are now composed almost entirely of shops and offices; but the other streets are still full of private houses, which is unusual for any city centre in Britain.

The New Town and the Old are divided and linked by Princes Street Gardens. These were once the old Nor' Loch, not finally drained until 1820. Once the private gardens of the householders of Princes Street, they are a welcome green space in the heart of the city. Bands play here in summer, and foot-sore tourists recover from struggling through the crowds of Princes Street.

Apart from being a beautiful city, Edinburgh is full of activity arising from its position as the capital of Scotland. At the east end of Princes Street, Old and New St. Andrews House hold the Scottish civil service and government departments. Scotland and England have completely inde-pendent legal systems, and the Scottish high court of justice is known as the Court of Session. This functions in a rather confusing huddle of buildings behind St. Giles. These include the old Parliament Hall. Edinburgh University has long outgrown the Old Quadrangle designed for it by Robert Adam, and its scientific, medical and engineering faculties are among the most important in Britain. The original engineer-ing faculty has now become a university in its own right, Heriot-Watt, in new buildings a few miles outside the city.

It would be impossible to list here all the fascinating things one can see or do in Edinburgh. There will be more details in Chapter Six. The Royal Mile alone would take several weeks to look at properly. Beginning from the top of the hill there is the Castle, and all the buildings which make it up; in the middle, St. Giles Cathedral, Parliament Hall, and John Knox's house; at the foot of the hill, Holyrood Palace and Abbey, and Arthur's Seat, a rocky hill in Holyrood Park. Bus tours run several times a day from Waverley Bridge, and there are guided tours on foot organised by the Scottish Tourist Board. But the best way is to wander down yourself, not forgetting to step aside into the fascinating wynds and closes, all of which have their own history. You can find a detailed guide to them in any Edinburgh bookshop.

In other parts of the city there are museums, art galleries, a zoo with a world-famous collection of penguins, a beautiful Botanic Garden, sports grounds, theatres – a hundred and one places for Edinburgh's half-million people and the thousands of visitors.

The tourist season is crowned by the Edinburgh International Festival, held in late August and early September, Music-lovers in particular flock to it from all over the world. During these three weeks Edinburgh is a cosmopolitan city that rises to the promise of its incomparable setting. By day, it is a bustling festival city, with banners fluttering over Princes Street. Every night it is transformed into something even more beautiful, as floodlighting picks out the Castle, the spires and domes and pillars, so that they seem to float by enchantment above our heads.

3 · Earning a Living

About one and a quarter million people live in the eastern Lowlands. Most of them are in the Greater Edinburgh area, that is, the land bordering the Forth basin.

After Glasgow, Edinburgh has the heaviest concentration of industry in Scotland. This may seem surprising, when we have said that Scotland's industrial belt stretches across the Midland Valley; but 'concentration' refers to the variety and density of industries within a given area.

Leith, Edinburgh's port, has the largest flour mills in the country. Most of the bread eaten in east Scotland is baked from the flour they produce. Edinburgh itself provides work in brewing, printing, and rubber-manufacture. Paper-making is important in areas not far from the city. This is to be expected, so near such an important centre of administration.

Most of the work-force is in the service-industries; that is, looking after the needs of a large body of people living in a small area. This covers transport, education, banking, business facilities, shops, sanitation, law and order, information, entertainment, etc. It also includes the moving about of manufactured goods – in fact, anything to do with the needs and luxuries of urban life, that does not actually involve making or manufacturing goods.

Tourism is now a very important part of the Scottish economy. Tourists spend more than three hundred million pounds per year in Scotland. In 1969 the Scottish Tourist Board was set up to look after tourism in Scotland. The STB is particularly concerned with the one million overseas visitors who come every year for the sake of Scotland's history and scenery. Encouraging hotels and restaurants is very important, as well as setting up information offices. Recently the STB has spent a lot of time and effort planning recreation facilities that will not spoil the uncrowded open spaces that are so attractive to native Scots as well as visitors. Carefully thought-out schemes have created a number of jobs in the remoter areas.

However, many of the people in the eastern Lowlands work in the traditional occupations. These are farming, fishing, textiles and mining.

About eighty-five per cent of Scotland's land is devoted to agriculture; but only a quarter of this is used for crops and grass. And most of the arable farms are on the eastern side of the country, from Berwickshire up to the Moray Firth.

On the whole they are mixed farms. They produce livestock and dairy goods as well as crops. The proportion of each depends on local conditions. Most of the dairying is carried on in central and south-western areas, where there is a higher rainfall. In eastern areas the livestock is sheep, beef and breeding cattle. Poultry and pigs are found too, but they are not so important.

There are only a few parts of Scotland where wheat can be grown. The Lothians is one of them. The wheat is what is known as a soft variety, and has to be mixed with hard grain from Australia or Canada before being milled for baking-flour. It is usually sown in early autumn. The main cereal crop, however, is barley. This is used by local breweries and distilleries, or sent to the seed-market. Sometimes it is used as feedstuff for animals, together with crops of oats. Since 1956 barley production in Scotland as a whole has risen from 218,000 to 855,000 acres.

Many Lothian farms use a six-year rotation system: oats;

potatoes; wheat; roots; barley; grass. This gives a good idea of their produce. The roots are used as winter-feed for the animals. The farms also go in for market-gardening of a mixed kind. Specialist market-gardening belongs more to other areas. For instance, there is tomato-growing in the Clyde valley, and soft fruit for jam is grown in vast quantities in Angus and Perthshire.

The same pattern of agriculture is found in Fife, although the soil is not so rich as in the Lothians. The red soil of East Lothian has been prized for over a thousand years. The Anglo-Saxon invaders were the first large-scale farmers here. They penetrated right up to the shores of the Forth and have left their mark in the many place-names ending in -*inge*, -*ingeham*, -*ham*, or -*ton*. Some people trace the markedly English character of the East Lothian villages right back to these early settlers. However, it probably has more to do with the fact that East Lothian was deeply involved in the eighteenth-century agricultural revolution.

Until then, the usual rural settlement was a *fermtoun* (in the Highlands called a *clachan*). This was not the same as a farm. It was a group of tenants who held possibly fifty acres in common. The land was divided into marginal *outfield*, occasionally cropped, but allowed to lie fallow most of the time, and the *infield*. The infield was the better land, but it was only one-fifth of the total area. It was usually sown year-about with oats and barley.

The fields were divided into S-shaped strips (*rigs*), each about half an acre in size. Every tenant would have his rigs scattered about the different fields, and they were re-distributed every year. This was to make sure that everyone had an equal share of good and bad land. There were no trees or hedges for shelter, and no one tried to grow any, because they might encourage birds which would harm the crops.

Between the rigs were wasteful banks or ditches. By modern

standards, the return on seed was incredibly poor, because the
soil was stony, undrained and cropped to exhaustion. The
huge wooden ploughs were normally drawn by oxen, not
horses. Eight to a dozen animals made a team. Four men were
needed to guide the whole clumsy operation of ploughing, and
even so, the soil was barely scratched.

Most of these tenants were on yearly leases, with no security,
although longer leases were sometimes granted in the south-
east after the 1620s. The tenants had no reason to improve
their smoky hovels, which were built of unmortared stone, and
thatched with turf. When they 'flitted' they often removed the
precious roof-timbers for their next dwelling.

In East Lothian conditions were not so bad as in the rest of
Scotland, but they were certainly bad compared with the
present state of this prosperous farming area. The Improvers
were landowners and farmers who introduced new ideas and
equipment to improve this situation. They began to drain and
enclose and lime the sour land, and introduced the rotation of
crops. They tried to persuade the tenants to take up these new
ideas by building them solid stone cottages, and granting
longer leases. They planted trees and hedges as wind-breaks,
and brought in new equipment, such as the iron swing-plough.
They were fiercely resisted at first, especially when they used
some of the precious ground to grow root-crops for animals.

Leading Improvers were Andrew Fletcher of Saltoun, and
the Earl and Countess of Haddington. John Cockburn of
Ormiston, already mentioned, is the most important of all. He
founded the Society of Improvers of Knowledge of Agriculture in 1723. Gradually these pioneers were followed by others
in the Borders and central Scotland. From 1747–55 a military
map of Scotland was produced on the large scale of one
thousand yards to one inch. It was drawn up by a military
engineer, William Roy. It shows the early stages, when
improvements were gradually creeping out from large estates

to the farming country round them. Forty years later, the Old Statistical Account of Scotland showed how much further the improvements had gone.

When the Improvers enclosed the fields they made them large. So on the whole they have not had to be redesigned for modern farm machinery, as has happened with the mediaeval field patterns in parts of England. Many Lowland farm buildings date from the late eighteenth century. Despite silos and modern extensions, the farming landscape of the Lowlands is still essentially the work of the Improvers.

If you look at a map you will see that apart from Fife, the Merse and East Lothian, most of the eastern Lowlands rises very quickly to hill country. The Lammermuirs and Cheviots hem in the Tweed basin; the Lothians rise into the Moorfoot and Pentland Hills, while in the counties of Peebles and Selkirk there are even higher hills that form the watershed of the Clyde and the Tweed.

On the lower slopes of these hills and the edge of the river-valleys there are upland farms that raise both crops and livestock. The lower ground is used for beef cattle, while sheep occupy the rough grazing above.

This is where the Forestry Commission is continuing the work begun by the Improvers, when they tried to renew the lost forests of Scotland. Over forty per cent of Scotland's present forest area has been planted since 1960. Although most of the Commission's land is north of the Highland Line, they give work to a good many people in the Lowlands as well. Timber is a crop as much as barley or oats, though a long-term one; the crop has to go through many processes before it is harvested. Forestry also supports other kinds of farming, since it provides shelter-belts for flocks and fields.

The modern Wood of Caledon has to please the tourist's eye as well as supply the new chipboard and pulping plants. The Forestry Commission has now been drawn into the tourist industry. Part of its work is to supply and manage camping-sites, nature-trails, and other outdoor pursuits to which it opens its land.

As you travel round the Borders you will see sheep grazing in sloping fields marked out by dry-stone walls that run down to the roadside. Further up, where the walls stop, you will see distant white dots busily grazing away right up to the summits of the hills, at nearly any time of the year.

7. Borders sheep: a ewe with her two lambs

Until the mid-eighteenth century most livestock was killed off in the autumn, and the carcasses salted. A few animals were brought indoors or herded into pens near the houses, to struggle through the winter in semi-starvation.

Then two things happened. Root-crops and artificial grasses began to be grown for winter-feed, and it became possible to keep a much greater number of animals alive through the winter. It was found, too, that sheep could be wintered on the hills – something thought impossible before.

As a result of these two developments there are now more sheep than people in Scotland. In the lambing season the number probably rises to eight million. The breeds are not quite the same as they were two hundred years ago, for then the sheep-farmers introduced new strains such as the Border Leicester, which was crossed with native hill-breeds.

The hill-farms specialise in sheep-rearing. They are set among the Cheviots, the great rolling hills of Tweeddale, and the ancient Ettrick Forest, all of them sheep areas from very early times. On the upper slopes you will find the native Cheviot breed, and the agile little Blackface, which terrifies motorists by scampering across unfenced moorland roads.

Life on these wind-swept hills has probably changed less than any other aspect of farming in the last century and a half. The rams are sent out to the ewes in late November; the lambing begins in mid-April, and the young sheep are clipped in June. The upland farms begin all this slightly earlier than the hill-farms, as conditions lower down are less bleak.

It was recently suggested by a research professor that some lambs might be imported from Afghanistan to cross with the little Blackfaces, which grow to a weight of about one hundred pounds. The result would be a sheep four times that weight, and the size of a donkey. The professor was quoted as saying, 'It might be better if, instead of taking domestic breeds from 'cushy' areas of the world, we thought of going to extreme environments'. This produced a tart reply from one Border shepherd, who offered to find the professor a month's work as a lambing assistant – 'To see whether he still thought Blackfaces lived in cushy country'!

When the railway came to the Borders there was a tremendous increase in the amount of livestock raised for meat. Before this, sheep and cattle could not be easily moved any great distance from their home area. Sheep, however, have always been reared in the Borders for their wool.

We have already seen how the monks shipped great quantities of it to the Continent. Later, most of it was spun and woven in the Borders, generally for local use. It was of poor quality. The Scottish Parliament passed acts to stop people importing the finer English cloth. At that time the Borders had a lot of wool available, and plenty of soft river-water to wash it. Apart from that, the region had no advantage over dozens of other places in Scotland where wool was spun at home and woven on hand-looms.

At the end of 1777 some weavers banded together to form the Galashiels Manufacturers' Corporation, to encourage the local cloth trade. They introduced machinery on a small scale, and improved their ways of marketing the cloth outside their own area. In 1803 Dorothy Wordsworth passed through Galashiels and noted in her journal that there was a 'manufactory' in the town. (In fact there were three.) But this meant only that there were some small sheds where the wool was sorted, then cleaned and carded by very simple machinery driven by water-power. The actual spinning and weaving was still done by people in their own homes. The 'mills' employed about fifty workers each.

This early use of water-power gave Galashiels, Selkirk, Hawick, and the other woollen towns a big advantage. Gradually other processes became mechanised. First came the spinning-jenny, in the early 1800s; then the mule, driven by water-power. These took over from the women's slower hand-wheel, and by 1833 all spinning had moved into the mills.

By then weavers were using Kay's flying shuttle. This allowed them to produce yard-wide cloth that would sell better in the English market. Previously, Scottish broadcloth had been only twenty-seven inches wide, and this is still the standard width for hand-woven Harris tweed.

It took much longer for weaving to move out of the workers'

homes into the mills. When it did, at first it too depended on water-power. This is why all the old mills in the woollen towns are built along the river-banks. But when the Edinburgh-Hawick railway opened in 1849 it was possible to use what are known as power-looms, because coal could now be brought in sufficient quantities from the Lothian coal field.

After the Napoleonic Wars checked cloth became popular in London. The fashion is supposed to have been started by Sir Walter Scott, who had his trousers made in black and white shepherd's plaiding. This cloth was woven by the *twill* method (in the Borders, *tweel*). Twill or tweel had a special weave: each thread crossed two others, not just one, which is the usual method. It is said that a London merchant, misreading the invoice on a parcel of cloth from the Borders, thought the label said *tweed*. So was born the name that is now given to almost all woollen cloth woven in Scotland.

Scottish wool was tough, but not of the softest quality. So the manufacturers began to buy wool from abroad, from Germany, Spain and Australia. This led to the second great industry of the woollen towns, fine Scottish knitwear that is prized all over the world. In Hawick they claim that this skill goes back to 1771, when a local magistrate introduced the first stocking-frames in Scotland. The modern knitwear industry is based entirely on imported wool. Lambswool comes from Australia; Cashmere, which is goat's hair, comes from China and India. From this is made the softest and most expensive luxury garments.

Fishing is another industry that has changed greatly over the years. Up until the late eighteenth century small fishing-craft were built and sailed from nearly every harbour along the eastern coast, as the Old Statistical Account tells us. The catch was white fish such as ling, cod and haddock. Most of the fishing was done with long, baited lines. At rivermouths,

8. Eyemouth harbour: one of the few south-eastern harbours of Scotland that are still important fishing bases

particularly the Tweed and the Eden, salmon was caught with stake-nets. All round the coast lobsters, crabs, oysters, and mussels (used for bait) also made up the catch. The boats were small, without decks, and of course driven only by sail.

At this time the herring fishing-grounds were almost monopolised by the Dutch, although a few Scottish boats operated from Crail and elsewhere. But after the Napoleonic Wars Scottish herring-fisheries began to boom. The Government gave grants of money to improve the harbours. One big drawback had been that most of the catch (of any kind) had to be smoked or pickled before it went bad. But when the railway came fresh herrings could be rushed by over-night express to the fish-markets of the south. Herrings continued to be fished all through the nineteenth century and later. But the herring shoals were moving further and further away, and during the Second World War they completely vanished from their old winter-grounds in the Forth.

Since 1953 there has been a move back to inshore fishing round the south-eastern coast of Scotland. Ring-nets and seine nets have now been added for trawling near the coast. Eyemouth is the most important harbour for this kind of fishing in the eastern Lowlands. Nearly half a million pounds was spent recently to re-equip the harbour, and a new fish-market was built. Deep-water trawling still goes on from Granton; but the Fife ports concentrate on what one might call 'restaurant' fishing – scallops, crabs and lobster. A factory for processing scampi and other seafood has been set up at Anstruther.

The pattern of success and decline in these eastern ports is a fascinating study, but much too complicated for this book. On the whole, a few big harbours have developed at the expense of the rest. Until the nineteenth century they were all tidal and fairly small. They all dealt in grain, salt, coal, salted fish, and imported timber and iron. But the Forth deposits a lot of sediment in its firth, particularly on its south side. This, with the geological features mentioned before, was a fatal drawback once Scotland entered the Industrial Age. Bigger ships with a quick 'turn-round' were needed, and larger harbours to take them. Most of the small ports found this too expensive, and they lost their harbour trade.

Since 1968 the whole Forth basin has been handled as the Port of Forth. The harbours concerned are Grangemouth, Leith and Granton on the south side, with Burntisland, Methil and Kirkcaldy on the north. The main products they handle between them are bauxite (used in making aluminium), coal, grain, wood-pulp, paper, chemicals, whisky, and petroleum.

The chief export of the Forth ports used to be coal, particularly for those in south-west Fife. The monks of Newbattle and Dunfermline were already mining coal in the thirteenth century. In 1435 an Italian traveller reported in amazement that poor people begging at church doors were overjoyed to receive stones as alms.

At first coal was taken from shallow pits or opencast workings. Conditions in the mines were horrifying. Until 1799 the Scottish miners were by law serfs, and their wives and children worked as hard as they did in the pits.

The black stone was so heavy it could be burned only near the pithead or shipped to customers. The East Lothian mines had to send coal to Leith before it could be used in Edinburgh. All coal carried in this way was 'sea-coal', and was taxed on leaving and entering a port. On the whole the Scottish tax was higher than the English, so it was cheaper for the Scots to burn coal sent from Newcastle. Scottish coal was exported from a very early time. By 1690 the Forth ports were sending sixty thousand tons a year to Amsterdam and Hamburg.

First-class coal was burned for fuel, and the second grade was used in manufactures. In the pre-industrial age this meant lime-burning (lime was needed for fertiliser, and the building-trade), distilling, glass-making, and evaporating sea-water to make salt. There were huge iron salt-pans all along the shores of the Forth – an industry that has completely vanished. It took six tons of coal to produce one ton of salt, so the amount of coal burned in this way was enormous. (Even so, the salt was suitable only for cooking and table use, and foreign salt had to be imported for curing meat or fish.)

In the late eighteenth century Carron Iron Works at Falkirk began to demand more and more coal from central Scotland. In the nineteenth, even more was needed for heavy engineering and steel-making. Coal was also sent overseas, mostly for steamships and railways. By the end of the 1930s Methil, the chief coal-port of Fife, had reached its peak of exporting three million tons a year. It seemed that the demand would go on for ever.

But since 1945 production has shrunk to fourteen million

tons a year, over the whole of Scotland. This is largely because in many ways oil has superseded coal. Half the coal mined in Scotland now goes to electricity-generating plants. Mining is concentrated in the best pits, and these have the most up-to-date equipment. Longannet in Fife is the largest electricity station in Britain, supplied from the most modern mine in Europe. Monktonhall pit in Midlothian supplies the power-station at Cockenzie, on the south side of the Firth of Forth. These two pits and Seafield, near Kirkcaldy, each produce about a million tons of coal a year.

The closing down of smaller pits, and the use of modern equipment, mean of course that fewer people are employed in the industry. As far as the individual worker is concerned, mining is a declining industry in Fife and the Lothians. In this way and others the pattern of employment has changed during the Seventies. There is also less work in farming. Berwickshire, for instance, now employs only half the number of people in farming that it did fifty years ago.

New industries in some places have sprung up to employ the surplus workforce. So at Eyemouth, a freezing and packing plant deals with the local vegetable produce. Dunbar has a large cement-works, evolved from the local lime-burning industry that has now become obsolete through the use of sprays and artificial fertilisers. In the Border towns, service centres have sprung up for the latest farm-machinery.

These new jobs do not appear by chance. Planning authorities now try to stop the smaller Lowland towns from becoming commuting 'dormitories' for the industrial Midland Valley and the great sprawl of Edinburgh. The new motor-ways and a vast increase in the number of private cars allow people nowadays to live further from their work. Planners are trying to bring in new industries that will persuade people to work as well as live in the less built-up areas. At the same time they have to see that the industries are not so large that they will ruin the small towns and their beautiful surroundings.

So in Fife and the Borders you will find small firms making precision tools, sports equipment, small plastic goods, printed material – and engaging in every kind of work that comes into the class of 'light engineering'. In the Borders a third new town, Tweedbank, is being set up on the lines of Glenrothes and Livingston. It can be expected to attract a lot of this new industry. In Bathgate, West Lothian, a newcomer is the truck and tractor plant set up by British Leyland in 1960.

So far the most important kind of new industry in the eastern Lowlands is electronics. The centre of it is at Glenrothes. As we have seen, this new town was planned as part of the revival of the Fife coal industry after World War II. But this did not happen.

Electronics began in Scotland with a wartime Ferranti plant in Edinburgh. Since then it has expanded enormously. There are about seventy firms making small parts and circuits for satellite and rocket systems, for computers, office-machines, and the instruments used in medical research. That is only a short list of some of the ways in which electronic technology is now used. Many of the firms are from overseas. They have been attracted to central Scotland for several reasons. The Government gives grants to encourage the building of new factories; there is a lot of industrial space for them in the new towns; there is a workforce no longer used by the shrinking older industries; and central Scotland has a large number of seats of higher education, where workers can be trained in the new skills. These places also have departments which specialise in the theory behind the new industry. Electronics depends on this kind of research to improve its methods and develop new systems. Glenrothes is within a ninety minutes' drive of seven universities.

Scotland has always had a severe 'brain-drain' problem. For three hundred years her most talented and energetic young people have been leaving to look for work in England or overseas. Electronics is one of the new fields of work which may eventually stop this happening.

Oil is another new industry that is closely linked with universities and technical colleges. Heriot-Watt has a Department of Off-shore Engineering, and a Department of Petroleum Engineering. The first deals with the technology of drilling in the North Sea, and the second with the nature of petroleum itself, and ways of making use of the vast deposits in the North Sea. The two sides are obviously very closely connected; the fact that the work is split into two separate departments shows how very important North Sea oil has become.

The world's first oil industry actually began in Scotland, close to the site of Livingston new town. There in 1850 James 'Paraffin' Young began producing crude oil from the shale that was mined locally. When refined, shale-oil, or paraffin, was burned in oil-lamps. The demand for it fell off when gas-lighting began. The shale industry has now completely vanished from the Lothian and Fife, leaving only its bings or tips to mar the landscape.

Shale-oil is basically the same substance as the oil used to produce petroleum, but it is at a different stage of the refinement. North Sea Oil was discovered when there was a search for gas under the southern part of the North Sea. The gas was discovered in 1965, and oil in 1969. Because of the savage weather, and the depth of the water, huge sums of money have to be spent on research and equipment before the oil can be brought ashore. First of all, oil-rigs drill the bed of the sea; when oil is found, permanent production platforms tap the well. The oil is brought ashore by pipeline or by special tankers. Both rigs and platforms have to be built on land and then towed out to their sites in the middle of the sea. They are very expensive to construct. Some of the platforms are almost as tall as the Eiffel Tower in Paris.

Only large international companies can afford to invest money on this scale. But a lot of the equipment and services needed by these companies can be provided by smaller firms. This is what is happening in the Forth area. So although Aberdeen is Scotland's 'oil capital' the eastern Lowlands are also affected by the new industry. Several local yards have turned from shipbuilding to producing and servicing equipment for the rigs and platforms. At Hound Point near the Forth bridges there is a terminal for crude oil piped from the Forties Field. The tankers that call in to collect it are very large – up to eighty thousand tons. British Petroleum intends eventually to send twenty million tons a year from Hound Point, mostly to the east coast of the USA. The average number of tankers calling at the terminal is twenty per month.

That is not the end of the story. The oil that gushes up from the sea bed is 'crude' – that is, it is mixed with various gases. Sometimes these are 'flared off' on the platform; but if they can be separated from the oil at various stages they too can be used commercially. The whole industry of petro-chemicals is built up on them.

When the gases are broken down they produce several vital modern substances: polythene, used in many household plastics; insecticides; the synthetic materials used in most of today's clothing; synthetic rubber; cosmetics; adhesives and detergents.

The biggest petro-chemical plant in Scotland is at Grangemouth, a few miles west of Lothian Region, on the Firth of Forth. It is also an important petroleum refinery, and has subsidiary plants in the Lothian Region. Grangemouth has plans to expand in the eighties, to become one of the biggest petro-chemical sites in Europe.

The crude oil from the sea can have some of its gases

removed on the production platform, if this is equipped in the proper way. The oil and the gases can be shipped to wherever they are needed at various stages in their separation. Each break-down stage needs a lot of expensive equipment, so it is sometimes more profitable to ship unseparated gases in a liquid form to other parts of the world. Special container ships are needed to do this, and already some Forth shipbuilders have plans to switch to this kind of work.

Petro-chemicals are likely to spread to Fife as well. The Shell/Esso Brent Field, north of Shetland, already pipes separated gases directly to the north of Scotland. There one kind of gas, methane, is removed and sold to British Gas for the national grid. It has now been suggested that the other liquid gases could be piped to a place in south Fife called Moss Morran. There a separation plant would produce two gases called propane and butane. They would be shipped from

9. Grangemouth petro-chemical plant: on the south shore of the River Forth, this is near the edge of Scotland's industrial belt

a tanker terminal at nearby Braefoot Point to North America. A later development would be yet another plant called an ethane cracker. This would produce ethylene, which again is one of the basic 'feedstocks' of the petro-chemical industry.

If this huge industrial development happened, it would in time give rise to a plant as large as Grangemouth. It would completely alter the appearance and the economy of south Fife. Many people feel that the area would be utterly spoilt by such a development; they are preparing to resist the Shell/Esso scheme.

On the other hand, unemployment is very high in south-west Fife, and a vast amount of export trade would be lost to Britain if the gases were not used.

These are some of the points that will have to be studied by the public enquiry commission that is going to look into the question. For it is not just a question of saving or spoiling a few miles of coastline. It is also about the best way to deal with the new industries and the ever-growing pressure they put on central Scotland at the end of the twentieth century.

4 · Transport and Communications

A modern map of Scotland shows a network of fairly new motorways and by-passes crossing the Midland Valley. The M8, the M9 and their feeder roads run over land that is, for Scotland, comparatively flat, and they serve very large communities. Two hundred years ago, these communities did not exist; and in any case the area was full of swamps and bogs that could be drained only with great difficulty.

The main routes across the Border follow the same ancient routes as they always have done. This is because traffic still has to cross the Southern Uplands by the hill-passes or the river valleys. Modern engineering can make firm foundations in ground that was once a swamp; but it cannot move mountains.

There are three main routes from England into Scotland. There is the eastern coastal road, the A1 or Great North Road. This is the longest, but the flattest. There is the western route by the Solway Firth. Once across the Border this splits into four separate routes up Nithsdale, Annandale, Eskdale and Liddesdale. These do not really concern us, being out of our area, except that a modern road, the A7, runs up Eskdale as far as Langholm, where it turns aside into Teviotdale and continues to Hawick. Near there it joins the central route which comes across Carter Bar. This is the A68, and it closely follows the line of Dere Street, the old Roman road, which has been traced up to Dalkeith in Midlothian. It was built by the governor of Britain, Gnaeus Julius Agricola, when he invaded southern Scotland. At that time the main Roman army was based at the three legionary camps of Caerleon-on-Usk, York and Chester. Agricola brought his troops up in two divisions. One marching from Chester, came up to Carlisle, then along the modern A74 route up Annandale to Crawford in upper Clydesdale. There it turned east to cross the Pentlands and reach the Forth at Inveresk. The other division came from York. Coming from Corbridge it crossed the Cheviots at High Rochester, passed the Eildon Hills (where it stormed a native fort), marched up Lauderdale, and probably over Soutra to the Lothian plain. There it joined the other division at Inveresk.

This 'pincer-movement' was the way Romans took over new territory. After the first advance forts would be built and manned along the route, the road would be properly surfaced, and minor link roads made for patrol parties, and bringing up supplies.

Agricola and later governors crossed the Forth to subdue tribes further north. They used the same system to build roads and forts in Fife and other parts of Scotland. But when the Romans withdrew from Scotland it was only Dere Street that remained in permanent use. In fact, it was the only properly surfaced road in Scotland for another fourteen hundred years.

At length it deteriorated into what it is today, a high grassy track. It was used on two fateful journeys: by James IV on his way to Flodden Field (1513) where the Scots were heavily defeated by the English and James himself was killed, and by Edward II heading towards Bannockburn (1314). In this battle Robert the Bruce routed an English army three times the size of his own, and Scotland achieved her independence.

The coastal route through Berwick-on-Tweed and Dunbar was dangerous for invaders. At Cockburnspath it is hemmed in between the Lammermuirs and the sea, and drops down steeply into a wooded valley. (The bridge built across it in

1837 was claimed at the time to be the highest in the world.) Nevertheless English armies came this way twice, in 1296 and 1546. They risked an ambush because they needed to keep in touch with the fleet that was carrying their supplies.

During the Middle Ages travellers walked or rode. Goods were carried by pack-horse or on the backs of pedlars. Anything too heavy for this was dragged along on sledges. So we must be careful not to think that roads in the modern sense existed. There were stony tracks or well-trodden paths; over flat ground they would spread out into wide stretches of caked mud or puddles. In wet or snowy weather they often could not be used at all. At all times of the year they were very difficult for wheeled vehicles.

An English state paper of 1543 mentions seventeen ways to cross the Cheviots. Among them are quaint names like Gamel's Path (Dere Street), Phillip's Cross, Redeswire, Wheel Causeway, and Hewghen Gate. These were used by the Border reivers. In their raids they shifted a huge amount of livestock and other gear, as the bitter complaints from their victims tell us. Most of these routes would now be called hill-paths.

When raiding finally stopped in the Borders, these paths and others further north were used by cattle-drovers. From 1750 there was a great cattle-market at Falkirk, called the Falkirk Tryst. It was held in the autumn. Most of the cattle were driven down from the Highlands. They were sturdy little black beasts, nowhere near the size of the beef Angus we rear today.

The main buyers were dealers from England. They arranged with the drovers to have the beasts herded to England to be fattened on the richer pastures there. Most of the cattle were then bought by the Navy Victualling Board. Salted meat was the only animal flesh that could be stored in the wooden warships, and only fattened cattle produced food good enough for the Navy. During the Seven Years War, the American War and later the Napoleonic Wars, there was a huge demand for Scottish cattle. But when the railways came, there was no need to drove cattle and the drove-ways ceased to be used. These paths are now the delight of hill-walkers.

The drovers did not want the roads to be improved: a hard surface was bad for the cattle's hooves. (If the animals had to go long distances on surfaced roads the drovers had them shod.) Other travellers were not so content. They complained about the pot-holes, the puddles, the constant breaking of wheel-axles. This was a common event, if any wheeled vehicle dared to jolt its way along the muddy, stone-littered tracks.

During the seventeenth century the Scottish Parliament passed several Acts about the roads. They ordered Justices of the Peace to make the men in each parish work six days a year on their local roads. This service was unpaid, so done very unwillingly, if at all. The system did not work very well. Strangely enough, the remoter Highlands had some two hundred and sixty miles of reasonably good roads. They had been built by General Wade after the 1715 Rising, the first attempt by the Jacobites to bring back the Stuart kings. Like the Roman roads, they were built for and by soldiers.

After 1750 the Turnpike system was used instead. This meant that a number of Trustees looked after the roads in their area. They paid for them by setting up toll-gates (called turnpikes) every so often at which everyone had to stop and pay a fee before the gate was opened. In Midlothian the charges were 'For every Horse with a Load . . . One Sixth Part of a Penny Sterling And for every Cart Waggon or Sledge passing laden or unladen . . . the Sum of One Halfpenny Sterling'.

Each area had to have a private Act of Parliament to set up its Turnpike Trust, so it took a long time for matters to improve. Between 1750 and 1800 three thousand miles of road were constructed in Scotland, three quarters of them after 1780.

The road-surface, however, was still very bad. At first people thought the best way was to use big stones with smaller pebbles filling the cracks. This was almost as bad as the old tracks, and very uncomfortable for passengers in coaches. Then the small stones were put as a separate layer on top, but the large stones worked their way through.

The problem was solved at last when an Ayrshire Trustee, John Loudoun Macadam, began breaking all the stones to the same size. 'Every stone which exceeds an inch in any of its dimensions is mischievous,' he wrote. Macadam also insisted on having skilled, well-paid labourers to build the roads. They had to put down a layer ten to twelve inches thick, resting on the natural subsoil. The road also had to be well drained.

Macadam experimented for fifteen years on his own local roads. At the beginning of the nineteenth century he became surveyor to many English Turnpike Trusts. His methods were adopted all over Britain; but he was not able to persuade the Government to go on to his next stage – to put road-making into the hands of some central office. This did not happen until 1937, when a Ministry of Transport took responsibility for main trunk roads in Britain.

The toll-gates were finally abolished in 1878. They were a great nuisance, since all traffic except the mail coaches had to stop at them. The charges also went up quite steeply from the early amounts mentioned for Midlothian. Sometimes you can still spot the toll-houses in which the gate-keepers lived, standing at the side of the road.

Milestones and direction posts were introduced into Scotland about 1765.

Here is a table of some travelling times to show how they gradually improved through the eighteenth and nineteenth centuries. They all refer to coach travel. Riders, especially if they used post-horses, could go much faster.

EDINBURGH to GLASGOW (forty-four miles)
1678 Coach with letters (not a regular service) six days
1749 Passenger coach: twelve hours
1800 Passenger coach: six hours
1827 Passenger coach: five hours

EDINBURGH to LEITH (one and a half miles)
1763 Hourly coach service: one hour
1783 Five or six coaches every half hour: fifteen minutes
(Better than the present bus service!)

EDINBURGH to LONDON (approximately four hundred miles)
1763 Monthly coach: twelve to sixteen days
1783 Stage coach: four days
1786 Stage coach: sixty hours
1830 Stage coach: forty hours

Improvement however was still very slow on minor roads.
In 1770 the carrier between Edinburgh and Selkirk took loads
of up to six cwt. The journey there and back took him a
fortnight, even in good weather. He used the dried-up bed of
the Gala Water in preference to the 'road'. Today, many of
these old roads are dual or three-lane carriageways; yet they
can still be blocked in winter by ice and snow.

When the roads were so bad it was often easier to travel by
water. In the eastern Lowlands this meant the Forth, the Tay,
and the lower reaches of the Tweed. Other non-tidal rivers
were mostly too fast or narrow to take regular water-traffic. In
any case much of the river-water was diverted to run mills of
various kinds.

The rivers could be dangerous to travellers trying to ford
them. Before 1764 there were only three bridges over the
hundred miles of the Tweed – at Melrose, Kelso, and Berwick-

on-Tweed. The Forth and Tay had ferry services from the earliest times. North and South Queensferry are named after Queen Margaret, who often used this crossing on her way to and from Dunfermline. Broughty Ferry, Earlsferry, and Ferry Port-on-Craig (now Tayport) are other obvious crossing-points, and there were still others, not so well known. This is why Pettycur, a tiny place in south Fife, appears on so many of the milestones there.

Apart from their overseas trade, the Forth ports used to handle a great deal of coastal traffic in the old days, carrying people and goods a few miles along the coast. This completely disappeared with the coming of the railways.

Because the Clyde, the Forth and the Tay wind deep into Scotland's central belt, canals were not of such urgent importance here as they were in England. However, the dream persisted of linking the Forth with the Clyde across the isthmus. This resulted in the Forth and Clyde Canal, opened in 1790 and not finally closed to traffic until 1963. In consequence Grangemouth became Glasgow's eastern port. There were several passenger services, but the canal was mainly used to carry grain and coal. Every year forty thousand tons of Lothian grain were sent to Glasgow.

The Union Canal ran from near Falkirk into the heart of Edinburgh. It was opened in 1822, and it too is now out of use. Two of the labourers on it were the body-snatchers Burke and Hare. The canal was used to bring coal and building materials into the city. The duty for canal-coal was one penny (about $\frac{1}{2}$p) a ton, as against three and sixpence ($17\frac{1}{2}$p) for sea-coal. We must remember that the 17p difference was even greater than it appears: at that time it could be several days' wages.

The canals were put out of use by the coming of the railways. In Scotland these started with the waggonways built to take coal from the pits to the nearest harbour. The waggons were moved by horses or merely the power of gravity, and the rails were usually made of wood.

One of the earliest waggonways was at Tranent in East Lothian (1722). The waggons ran down with coal to Cockenzie harbour; and horses pulled them back up the slope, loaded with cargoes from the Scandinavian ships that called at the harbour. This route was used by one of the columns of Prince Charlie's army when it defeated General Cope at the Battle of Prestonpans (1745).

Another early line was the Charlestown Railway which took coal from Dunfermline to Rosyth (1767). Sometimes it also took passengers to catch the Granton-Stirling packet-boats there.

In 1817 a steam locomotive was used on the Kilmarnock-Troon waggonway; but at first the railway were thought of as being only a feeder system for the canals. In 1824 the editor of the *Scotsman* newspaper forecast a network of railways with steam locomotives that would carry passengers between every large town in Scotland. At the time this was received in much the same way as the forecasts of space travel in early science fiction. But in the 1830s railway fever began to grip Lowland Scotland, and profoundly changed the lives of everyone.

A separate Act of Parliament was needed to set up each line. A number of small companies developed, each trying to beat its rivals in the vast market that now lay open. There was great excitement when work on a new track started; and huge crowds stood cheering the first trains along the line.

The Edinburgh and Glasgow opened on 21st February 1842. There were gala trains leaving each city with a thousand passengers. Large quantities of champagne and claret were consumed! The running of Sunday trains brought great protests. A pamphlet was published called *Railway Travelling on the Lord's Day Indefensible*, and ministers of religion led prayers on Waverley Station, trying to persuade passengers to give up their wicked ways. The first two Sunday trains were withdrawn; it was some time before they were run again.

When the fuss had died down, the Edinburgh and Glasgow settled into a four-times-daily service in each direction. The journey took two and a half hours. Fares were: first class eight shillings (40p); second class (seats but no windows) six shillings (30p); third class (no seats and open trucks) four shillings (20p). Though these fares seem cheap, in terms of what money could buy in the mid-nineteenth century they represent about ten times the present-day fare.

The railway linked Edinburgh with Dunbar in 1846 and with North Berwick in 1850. The Edinburgh and Hawick opened in 1849. As we saw in Chapter 3, this made an enormous difference to the woollen towns. Now they could draw on the Lothian coal-field. Various cross-branches soon linked Kelso, Selkirk, Galashiels, Jedburgh and Peebles. The lines were used for coal and cattle, as well as passenger services. Fife, too, soon became covered with a network of railway tracks.

The two great rivals were the Caledonian and North British. Between them they swallowed up most of the smaller companies. The Caledonian was set up in 1845 to run the line between Carlisle and Glasgow. After setting up a link-line from Carstairs to Edinburgh it began to invade the territory of its eastern rival, the North British. At one time the struggle led to fifty-four trains a day running between Glasgow and Edinburgh – most of them empty! The Caledonian finally retreated from east Scotland, but the two companies' enormous railway hotels, the North British and the Caledonian, still glare in rivalry from opposite ends of Princes Street.

In the nineteenth century the railway could not possibly be beaten for speed on long journeys. As early as 1850 you could

10. Forth Rail Bridge: built in the late nineteenth century, it makes a striking contrast to the modern road bridge in the background

travel between Edinburgh and London in twelve hours. The next year, day-excursion tickets were being offered for the Great Exhibition at Crystal Palace. In the eighties the London–Edinburgh or Glasgow run was reduced to eight and a half hours. There was greater comfort, too: dining-cars, sleepers, gas lighting, and proper heating in winter.

One famous event of the railway age was the great railway race to the north in August 1895. This was between locomotives using the west and east coast routes from London to Aberdeen (well over five hundred miles.) The times were eight hours thirty-two minutes for the west and eight hours forty minutes for the east. Such high speeds were unusual, of course.

Two great monuments of this age lie within our area. The Forth Railway Bridge was built between 1883 and 1890 to take the main line to Aberdeen. It is 8,295 feet long, a network of dull red girders, in a triple diamond shape. Using fifty tons of paint, twenty men take three years to paint it. Then they have to start again!

Compared with this, the Tay Bridge is rather dull to look at. It was built between 1871 and 1877 and was 10,620 feet long. This was the first Tay bridge. It was a continuous run on pillars with a section in the middle known as 'the high girders'. When Queen Victoria travelled across it in 1879 she was very impressed. She gave the engineer a knighthood. A few months later, on Sunday, 28th December, there was a terrible storm in Fife. The train from Edinburgh had just reached the centre of the bridge when the high girders collapsed. The train crashed into the Tay, and over a hundred lives were lost. 'The Tay Bridge Disaster' has become one of those events that stir people's imagination. There have been several books and television programmes about it.

A second bridge, even longer – over two miles – began to be built in 1881. When finished, it was more thoroughly tested than any bridge had ever been. It is the railway bridge now in use.

British railways were nationalised in 1948. Since 1963, after the Beeching Report, more and more branch lines and stations have been closed. In our area there now survive only: the main Edinburgh-London line, with a branch to North Berwick; Edinburgh-Glasgow; Edinburgh-Dundee; and Edinburgh-Perth. These last two provide some rail services through Fife. All the Border and Fife branch lines have been closed. Whatever happened to the great railway age?

What happened was that other forms of transport took over from the railways, as the railways once took over from the stage-coaches. As with the coal industry, money has been spent on concentrating a few main services and making them super-efficient. The Edinburgh-Glasgow run on the electrified line has been reduced to forty minutes.

In the 1890s there were attempts to set up suburban

railways on the fringes of large cities. Except in Glasgow, this was foiled by the growth of the electric tram-car system. Then, after World War I (1914–18), ex-servicemen bought up surplus army trucks and lorries and began to run local bus services. Over short distances these were faster and more convenient than trains, and could put passengers down nearer their homes.

Since World War II (1939–45) there has been a great increase in road transport. Lorries and containers now carry many of the goods that were once sent by rail. Private cars, too, are much more widely owned than they were before the war. This has caused, and partly been caused by, a much greater scatter of population outside the old city centres. The railway stations are often too far away from the new suburbs and housing developments to be useful even if the trains were still using them.

In the city centres, however, the increased motor-traffic has caused serious problems. It is so difficult to find parking space for all these vehicles that people have discovered that the advantages of private transport for shopping and driving to work are quickly disappearing. On the other hand, public transport is slow and unreliable, owing to the multitude of other vehicles on the streets. So far, no one has been able to solve this problem.

Since 1955 the roads outside cities have also become more crowded, especially in the summer season. This has resulted in great pressure on the Government to improve the roads. To shorten journey-times, two toll-bridges have been built. These are across the Forth and the Tay, both of them near the earlier railway bridges. The Tay Road Bridge is impressive for its length (nearly one and a half miles) rather than its appearance. Bridging the Tay seems to be associated with disaster: the construction engineer, William Logan, was killed in an air-crash shortly before the bridge was completed. It was opened in 1966.

The Forth Road Bridge was opened by the Queen in 1964. It is suspended from cables; its graceful span makes a striking contrast with the dense meshwork of the older railway bridge. It has a pedestrian walkway and a large motel with a car-park. Crowds of sight-seers come to it every weekend. They also go to South Queensferry, where they cluster round the jetty once used by the old steam ferry. The nearby Hawes Inn is featured in R. L. Stevenson's *Kidnapped*.

These two road bridges have had a great effect on the industry and population of Fife. Many people now commute from their homes there to work in Dundee and Edinburgh. The Kingdom has lost its old isolation, but not, so far, the charm of its small towns and villages.

One of Scotland's two major civil airports is just outside Edinburgh at Turnhouse. There is also an RAF base at Leuchars in Fife. Turnhouse has just acquired a new runway to fit it for increased jet traffic. It has inter-city flights to Glasgow, London, and other British cities, but its main traffic is in Continental and American jet-flights. These serve chiefly the tourists that pour into Scotland every summer.

5 · Famous People

Edinburgh alone has connections with nearly every famous man or woman that Scotland has produced. To go through all of them – not to mention others more closely linked with Fife, the Lothians, or the Borders – would need a book several hundred pages long. In this chapter only a few can be included.

Mary, Queen of Scots has been mentioned several times, but there is another famous queen who spent far longer in Scotland. Queen Margaret (*c.* 1046 – 1093) belonged to the royal house of England. She was born in Hungary, where her father had been exiled. There he married a German princess. When Margaret was about ten years old her father was invited back by Edward the Confessor, but the Norman Conquest forced Margaret with her brother and sister to flee to the Scottish court. She married the Scottish King Malcolm III in about 1069. Malcolm himself had spent many years in England, though this was before Margaret came back from exile. So both Margaret and Malcolm brought a strong English influence into Scotland. They paved the way for the Anglo-Norman feudal society that was set up by their youngest son, King David I.

There were six sons and three daughters from this marriage. Margaret named all her sons after men of her own family or biblical characters. Three sons became Kings of Scotland; and her three daughters all married into other royal families.

She spent much of her time trying to reform the Scottish

Church. The Culdees had many practices that were quite different from those of the Church of Rome. Margaret did not try to suppress the Culdees; her own reforms were very mild. She changed some of the ritual in the Mass, and altered the date when Lent began. She also sent for Benedictine monks from Canterbury, and built a house and church for them near the palace in Dunfermline, in about 1074. These acts, though slight, were very important. They led to a complete change in the Scottish Church, and a flood of religious foundations in later reigns.

Margaret's life-story was told by her confessor Turgot. From him we learn that King Malcolm used to have his wife's prayer-books decorated with precious stones. This was the only way he could show his respect for her piety: he was unable to join her devotions, because he could not read.

Malcolm was often away fighting the English. He invaded England five times. On 13th November 1093 he was trapped at Alnwick and killed with his eldest son. Three days later, when the news reached Queen Margaret, the Anglo-Saxon Chronicle tells us, 'She was distressed even to death, and . . . gave up her spirit'. She had died in Edinburgh Castle, and her body was taken to Dunfermline, to be buried in the church she had built.

'Margaret' is still a favourite girl's name in Scotland. The queen was proclaimed a saint in 1249. She was Scotland's only canonised saint until 1976, when St. John Ogilvie, a Jesuit burned in 1604, in Glasgow, was canonised. When Robert the Bruce decided to destroy Edinburgh Castle rather than let it fall into English hands, the only building he left standing on the Rock was the little chapel of St. Margaret.

The famous Reformer John Knox was a native of Haddington in East Lothian. He is often said to be responsible for the *dourness* or grim gloom of Scottish life in later centuries – usually by those who know little about him. In fact, both the social attitudes and the religious doctrine that are linked (rightly or wrongly) with Calvinism – the creed followed by the Scottish Church – were brought in by later Reformers. Knox's last wish was for the Scottish Church to have bishops; and he told Queen Mary that he did not 'utterly condemn' dancing. Both these views would have got him into serious trouble with the Kirk Sessions a hundred years later!

After studying at Glasgow and possibly St Andrews as well, Knox became a notary – a kind of secretary – attached to the diocese of St. Andrews. He became a follower of the Reformer George Wishart, who was burnt for heresy in 1546 at St. Andrews. Wishart's supporters then murdered Cardinal Archbishop Beaton, who had ordered the burning. Then they shut themselves up in the Castle, where they had killed the Cardinal. Knox joined them, for his own safety. Rather oddly, he was also tutoring some sons of Lothian lairds at the same time, inside the Castle. The garrison were impressed by his lessons, and bullied Knox into preaching in their support in the parish church. When first asked to do this, Knox 'brust furthe in maist aboundant tearis'. He soon gained confidence, as his later career shows.

The French fleet arrived and forced the Castle garrison to surrender. John Knox had to work for a year and a half in its war-galleys. After this he spent a lot of time in England and abroad, helping when he could the movement that was growing in Scotland against France and the Church of Rome. He returned to Scotland in 1559, and preached a sermon at Perth that led to the looting of religious houses. So he was at the very centre of things when the eighteen-year-old Mary Stuart returned in 1561 to become Queen of Scots. Although officially queen since the age of one week, she had been married as a child to the eldest son of the king of France, but he died before his father, and Mary came back to her native Scotland.

In his *First Blast of the Trumpet Against the Monstrous Regiment of Women* Knox had tactlessly written against female rulers. 'Regiment' here means 'government'. For this Queen Elizabeth had refused to let him return to England.

Mary summoned Knox to an interview in Holyrood Palace. He tried to back down by claiming his book had been written only 'against that wicked Jesabell of England', but he stood his ground when he argued with her about the Roman Catholic and Protestant faiths. The Reformation had been officially established in Scotland in the previous year by the *Confession of Faith*. An Act had been passed by the Scottish Parliament, but of course it had to be signed by the ruler – Mary, a Roman Catholic. The Queen never did this; instead, she issued a proclamation saying in effect that she would not interfere with her subjects' religion if they would not interfere with hers.

Knox and the Reformers could not accept this. Mary's brief and stormy reign ended in disaster, made worse by the scandals surrounding her second and third marriages, with Lord Darnley and the Earl of Bothwell. She fled from Scotland, never to return, in May 1568.

In 1560 Knox had also helped draft a *Book of Discipline*. This laid down how the new reformed Church should be run; but it also made detailed proposals on the running of schools and universities. It had suggestions about pensions and allowances and other matters, some of which were not heard of again until the rise of the Welfare State in 1945.

Unfortunately these new ideas would have proved very expensive to put into practice. The money would have had to come from the revenues of the old Church. Many of these had already beeen seized (under the pretext of reform) by people who had no intention of giving them back. So Knox's suggestions were not accepted.

Apart from this one disappointment it seemed that his work was now secure. He preached at Stirling at the coronation of the infant King James VI, Mary's son. But in 1570 Knox's patron, the Regent Moray, was assassinated, and war between Protestants and Roman Catholics broke out again. In 1572, before this was settled, Knox died, not living to see later events that led to the Union of the Crowns. Knox was buried in the churchyard of St. Giles, where he had preached so many sermons. His grave is supposed to be marked by the brass initials now set into the paving stones outside the church.

In 1574 a second *Book of Discipline* was drawn up by Andrew Melville. He, more than Knox, is really the founder of the kind of Presbyterianism followed by the modern Church of Scotland.

The wars between Scotland and England during the period from the thirteenth to the sixteenth century involved the whole civilian population of southern Scotland. In the early War of Independence the Countess of Buchan, who had crowned Robert the Bruce at Scone, was hung over the walls of Berwick-on-Tweed in an iron cage. After several years of being a public spectacle, she died. The Bruce's sister suffered the same fate at Roxburgh, but she lived to be set free after the Battle of Bannockburn in 1314.

After the Bruce died, Scotland was ruled by Randolph, Earl of Moray. He was Regent for the young David II. Then the Regent died too, and English troops overran southern Scotland after the Battle of Halidon Hill, in 1333.

The English naturally tried to capture all the major castles. One of the most important was the Castle of Dunbar. The Earl of Dunbar was fighting elsewhere, and the castle was commanded by 'Black Agnes', the twenty-five-year-old Countess, who was the daughter of the dead Regent. She was given this nickname because of her dark hair.

Dunbar Castle stood on high rocks overlooking the sea. The English army commander, the Earl of Salisbury, closed it with a cordon of troops. He also had two Genoese galleys patrolling the sea.

Salisbury attacked the fortress every day with catapults that threw huge stones at the battlements. Black Agnes walked around the castle wall, jeering at these attacks. When one of the stones hit the battlements, she and her maids used to go round with small towels wiping off the dust raised by the stones.

Even her enemies admired the spirit of the young Countess. An English minstrel wrote:

> She kept a stir in tower and trench,
> That brawling, boisterous Scottish wench.
> Came I early, came I late,
> I found Agnes at the gate.

Salisbury tried another kind of siege-engine, a 'sow'. This was a wooden shed on wheels that protected soldiers trying to break through the base of a wall. As the shed trundled up Agnes stepped on to the parapet and shouted:

> 'Beware, Montagow,
> Farrow shall thy sow!'

This was the signal for a huge rock to be dropped over the wall. Some soldiers were crushed, and Black Agnes shouted out more insults as the survivors scuttled away.

Once Salisbury was riding near the walls with a knight who was shot dead by an archer on the battlements. The Earl is said to have remarked, 'Black Agnes's love-shafts pierce to the heart!'

When it became obvious that the assault on the Castle would not work Salisbury had Agnes's brother brought from his prison in England and paraded him in front of her. He threatened to kill him, if she did not hand over the Castle. Whatever she felt, Agnes called his bluff: she dared him to go

on, saying the only effect would be to make her heiress to the
Earldom of Moray. Salisbury did not have the cruelty to carry
out his threat.

The English army then sat down to starve out the garrison.
After five months, they had run out of food completely and it
seemed as if all Agnes's brave efforts to keep up the morale of
her followers had been useless. But at this point Sir Alexander
Ramsay and forty men managed to get into the Castle secretly
by the Water Gate. The next morning they made a surprise
attack on the English camp. Despite their small numbers they
inflicted a serious defeat on their enemies. The Earl of Salisbury
decided to give up the siege, and the two sides made a truce.

With so many harbours and such a long coast-line this area has
naturally produced many famous sailors. James IV and James
V both enlarged the Scottish navy. At that time trading ships
and warships were not really distinct classes. The three Barton
brothers of Leith were all notable merchants and privateers,
and caused a lot of annoyance to Henry VIII of England. Sir
Andrew Wood was commander of the *Great Michael*, built in
1512, 'sa stark and thik that na canon could gang throw hir'.
He too harried English shipping. Henry VIII offered an
annual pension of £1,000 to anyone who would take Sir
Andrew prisoner.

Tempted by this an English captain, Steven Bull, lay in wait
'at the bak of May' with three ships. (The Isle of May is at the
entrance to the Firth of Forth.) He knew that Sir Andrew was
returning from the Low Countries with two vessels. When the
English bore down on him Sir Andrew made a stirring speech
to his sailors, then joined battle with 'artaillzie and the croce-
bowis . . . lyme pottis and fyre ballis . . . and twa-handit
swerdis'. They were so near land that 'all the men and women
that dwalt neir the coast cam and beheld the fechting'.

Night parted them, but in the morning they fought again.

The south wind had already kept them fighting all the way from St. Abbs Head to the mouth of the Tay. Now the Scots redoubled their efforts; they captured the three English ships, and towed them triumphantly to Dundee.

Even in retirement Sir Andrew did not give up the water entirely. He had a canal dug between his house and the church, so that he could sail to Mass!

The most famous sailor of all is Alexander Selkirk, the son of a Largo shoemaker. You can see his statue above a house in the town. Daniel Defoe probably heard about him when he was up in Scotland. He turned his adventures into the famous tale of *Robinson Crusoe*.

The Anglo-Scottish Wars left little time for art or literature. There are a few shadowy figures who wrote chronicle histories in prose or verse, such as Andrew Wyntoun (1355–1422), John Barbour (1320–1395), Walter Bower (1385–1449), and John Major (1470–1550). (All the dates are approximate.) They are connected with the eastern Lowlands through the positions they held in the Scottish Church, though some of them were also natives of the area.

Under the later Stuarts occurred the brief Scottish Renaissance. George Buchanan (1506–1582) scholar and Latin poet, held several Church positions, including one as Principal of St. Leonard's College in St. Andrews. In his own time he was a European rather than a Scottish figure. Sir Robert Lindsay of Pitscottie (1532–1580), the historian already quoted on Andrew Wood, and Sir David Lindsay of the Mount (1486–1555) were probably related, and were both Fife lairds. Sir David Lindsay is best known for *Ane Satyre of the Thrie Estaitis*. This is a long morality play that calls for reform among all classes of society. Its homely scenes and vivid Scots phrases have led to it being revived twice in the Edinburgh Festival.

Gavin Douglas (1472–1522), Provost of St. Giles, made a Scots translation of the *Aeneid* of Virgil. This was not published until 1533. William Dunbar (1460–1524) wrote some sharp, satiric pieces based on his close contact with the court of James IV. Robert Henryson (1430–1500) was a schoolmaster of Dunfermline. He wrote some quaint Scots versions of Aesop's fables, and other pieces, including his famous *Testament of Cresseid*.

Round about 1600 there were several good minor poets who belonged to south-east Scotland. The best known is William Drummond (1585–1649) of Hawthornden in Midlothian. Ben Jonson visited him in 1618, walking all the way from London. When the two poets met, they burst into rhyme: 'Welcome, welcome, royal Ben!' 'Thank ye, thank ye, Hawthornden!'

During the Covenanting seventeenth century, there was not much encouragement for creative writers. Many famous books of divinity were produced, but they are not read a great deal nowadays except by theologians.

In the eighteenth century some very well-known figures emerge. Robert Burns is the best-known, but he has little connection with eastern Scotland, except for a few visits. Burns owed a great deal to two Edinburgh poets, Allan Ramsay (1686–1758) and Robert Fergusson (1750–1774). They both used the six-line stanza that is associated with Burns, as in the well-known *Lines to a Fieldmouse*.

Ramsay was a wig-maker in the High Street, but became rich enough to give this up, and built himself an oddly-shaped house just below the Castle. Its site is still known as 'Ramsay Gardens'. He collected four volumes of old English and Scottish songs, *The Tea Table Miscellany*, (Burns later adapted many of them) and he wrote a dramatic pastoral in five acts, *The Gentle Shepherd* (1725).

Robert Fergusson went to Edinburgh High School and then St. Andrews University, meaning to study for the Church.

After four years he gave up this idea and spent the rest of his life as a clerk in Edinburgh, copying out official documents. He found the work very tedious, and relieved his boredom in two ways: by heavy drinking in Edinburgh's social clubs, which met in the city taverns, and by writing about the scenes and characters of Edinburgh in sparkling, vigorous Scots verse.

From January 1772 to the end of 1773 one or two long poems appeared every month in *The Weekly Magazine, or, Edinburgh Amusement*. Fergusson's hectic life and intense creative effort burned him out. He became ill and fell into a mental state then labelled 'melancholia'. He was moved to an asylum, and apparently committed suicide on 17th October 1774.

When Burns visited Edinburgh he generously repaid his debt by raising a stone over Fergusson's unmarked grave in the Canongate churchyard.

Fergusson's old Scots words make his verse difficult for us today. This is a pity, for it contains the most vivid picture of eighteenth-century Edinburgh. Try reading aloud these two stanzas from 'Caller (fresh) Oysters'. This is how he describes the awful autumn rain, and the cosiness of an old tavern. I have modernised the spelling.

> When big as burns the gutters rin,
> Gin ye hae catched a droukit skin,
> To Luckie Middlemist's loup in,
>   And sit full snug
> O'er oysters and a dram of gin
>   Or haddock lug.
>
> When auld Saint Giles, at eight o'clock,
> Gars merchant lowns their shoppies lock,
> There we adjourn with hearty folk
>   To birle our bodles
> And get wharewith to crack our joke,
>   And clear our noddles.

The late eighteenth and early nineteenth centuries produced many famous writers: Sir Walter Scott, Thomas Hogg ('The Ettrick Shepherd'), and the editors and contributors to the famous *Edinburgh Review* and *Blackwood's Magazine*. Of the philosophers, historians and economists, two are world-famous.

David Hume (1711–1776) was the son of the laird of Ninewells, in Berwickshire. His famous *Treatise of Human Nature* was published from 1738–40 and is one of the key books in European philosophy. Hume spent a lot of time in London and France but eventually settled in Edinburgh. Everyone liked him, even the ministers who were horrified by the ideas of 'the Great Atheist'. The name 'St. David's Street' was chalked up outside his house by an anonymous joker – and stuck. The street runs off St. Andrew's Square, at the east end of Princes Street.

The most famous native of Kirkcaldy was Adam Smith (1723–1790). Like Hume he worked and travelled outside Scotland but eventually came to settle in Edinburgh, after publishing *An Enquiry Into the Nature and Causes of the Wealth of Nations* in 1778. This book was the beginning of political economy. It put forward the revolutionary idea that a nation's wealth is not its gold and silver, but its raw materials, which can be converted into goods for trade. William Pitt was greatly influenced by Smith's book when he was Prime Minister.

Hume and Smith were among the greatest minds of their age, but they led remarkably simple lives. Hume's hobby was cooking; his friends were often invited to suppers he had cooked himself. Adam Smith was notoriously absent-minded, and stories about his 'adventures' constantly amused his friends. One day in Kirkcaldy, while he was writing his famous book, he went to think over some problem in the garden, still wearing his dressing-gown. Pacing along, he lost all sense of time and place. When the problem was solved, he was startled

11. Self-portrait of Allan Ramsay,
the eighteenth-century Edinburgh painter

to hear church-bells ringing above his head. He had walked
the fifteen miles into Dunfermline!

Scott, Stevenson and John Buchan are three famous writers
connected with the Borders and Edinburgh; but they have
been written about in other books, so we will pass on to the
artists.

The first well-known Scottish artist was Allan Ramsay
(1713–1784), son of Ramsay the poet. He painted the leading
men and women of Edinburgh; but in 1756 he moved to

London and became a court painter. Sir Henry Raeburn (1756–1823) stayed at home, except for some years of study in London and Rome. He is supposed to have produced about six hundred of his fine and elegant portraits. They are narrow in their social range, but they are the most vivid reminder of the people who made early nineteenth-century Edinburgh 'the Athens of the North'.

Sir David Wilkie (1785–1841) was son of the minister of Cults in Fife. He delighted in painting the ordinary people of Scotland, and is famous for the vast number of faces he put on each canvas. Two of his best-known works are *Pitlessie Fair* and *The Penny Wedding*. He went on to paint famous historical events. Many of his pictures used to be used as illustrations in history text-books.

The Scottish Lowlands have produced a number of famous scientists and mathematicians. John Napier of Merchiston (1550–1616) tried to invent a hydraulic screw to drain coal-mines, a burning-mirror that would destroy enemy ships, and other ingenious devices. He actually did make the first calculating machine for multiplication and division, and is the inventor of logarithms. Puzzled by all this, people of his day accused him of being a wizard.

Timothy Pont (1565–1614) of Edinburgh, was the first person to survey Scotland and produce reasonably accurate maps of it. James Hutton (1726–1797), a Berwickshire laird, is connected with the Improvers. He is better known as the author of *Theory of the Earth*. In this he suggested that the earth had a 'crust'; so he is the founder of modern geology.

The famous engineers of this age, such as James Watt and Thomas Telford, really belong to another part of the country. But James Taylor (1723–1825) and Henry Bell (1767–1830) both have connections with south-east Scotland. They were both pioneers in using steam to propel ships, although both found their ideas accepted in America before they were made great use of in their own country.

The list of scientists and physicians would be endless. Mary Somerville (1780–1872) has been called 'the most remarkable woman of her generation'. In her lifetime there were no university research departments or laboratories, and as a woman she was in any case cut off from any experimental work that existed. She managed however to study and write on astronomy, physical geography, chemistry, and physics so brilliantly that she won high honours from many learned societies. She was married twice, both times to her cousins. Her first husband was the son of an Admiral in the Russian navy, but his family came from south Fife, where Mary spent a lot of her girlhood, observing wild life on the beaches. He died young, and she married, six years later, her cousin William Somerville, who came from Jedburgh, where she herself had been born. William Somerville was an army surgeon. After his marriage he held back his own career so that his wife could follow through her scientific researches. Mary Somerville published her last work in her eighty-ninth year. Somerville College, the women's college in Oxford, is named after her.

Edinburgh can claim many distinguished people in the field of medicine. Alexander Monro was the name of three generations of Professors of Anatomy. Alexander (1697–1767) was the real founder of the University's medical and surgical school. His fame as a teacher drew pupils from far outside Scotland. Alexander (1733–1817) was the most brilliant of the three, both in research, which brought him a European reputation, and as a lecturer. Alexander (1773–1859) had as his rival Dr. Knox of the Royal College of Surgeons, who also lectured in anatomy, and was involved with Burke and Hare in the great body-snatching scandal of Edinburgh in the early nineteenth century.

Sir James Young Simpson (1811–1870) was one of the greatest physicians of the age. He is best known as the person who first used chloroform as an anaesthetic. On 28th November 1847 he experimented on himself and two other doctors. The three 'sat each with a tumbler in hand, and in the tumbler a napkin. Chloroform was poured upon each napkin, and inhaled. Simpson . . . after a while, was roused by Dr. Duncan snoring, and by Dr. Keith kicking about in a far from graceful way'.

This amusing incident marked one of the greatest steps forward in medicine. Before then, surgical operations and sometimes childbirth had involved severe pain and suffering. The new discovery was at first violently opposed by some churchmen. They said it was interfering with the laws of Providence. But gradually its use became accepted.

Another famous Edinburgh doctor is Elsie Inglis (1864–1917). She lived at a time when women were struggling to be admitted into the profession of medicine. This led to her taking part in the Suffrage movement, for at that time no married woman could have an operation without her husband's consent. She was horrified by a case where one of her patients was condemned to a painful and lingering death because the woman's husband refused to let her go into hospital on the grounds that there would be no one to look after the children.

Dr. Inglis's work was mainly among the poorer people of Edinburgh. She founded the first maternity hospital there, which gave special training to women medical students. This led to a children's clinic, and the use of district nurses. Dr. Inglis also persuaded the Town Council to subsidise research work on nutrition. All this is commonplace today, but very new at the time.

Her work in Edinburgh was just as important as her setting up of the Scottish Women's Hospital Units in World War I, although this is what she is famous for. The army medical officer at Edinburgh Castle, to whom she first offered her idea told her to 'go home and sit still'. She persisted, and the Units saw service in France and Serbia (now north-eastern Yugoslavia), and Russia. Dr. Inglis exhausted herself by her work in the overcrowded military hospitals and died on her way home, in a hotel at Newcastle.

6 · Holidays and Visits

In this chapter and the next we shall be thinking about the interesting things one can do or look at in the eastern Lowlands. Some of the suggestions involve quite a lot of active searching-out; but on the whole this chapter will deal with places and buildings, and the next will be about energetic pursuits like ski-ing, sailing and walking.

If you are on holiday in a certain area there are two ways you can spend your time. You can enjoy things as you come across them, or you can follow a 'theme' holiday. In either case it really depends on you how much information you try to find out before you begin your holiday.

The Scottish Tourist Board publishes pamphlets on Sir Walter Scott and Mary Queen of Scots, describing places associated with these two famous characters. There is another pamphlet on stately homes, another on churches, and a rather unusual one, which perhaps belongs to the next chapter, called *Scotland at Work*. This gives a list of places where you can go to watch people working – distilleries, woollen mills, glass-works, potteries, and other craft workshops. The longer visits give you a guided tour as well. You can of course choose your own 'theme' – battles, castles, or anything else that interests you.

Whatever kind of holiday you choose, here is a description of some interesting things you may want to include in it.

Outside London, Edinburgh probably has the largest number of museums of any city in Britain. The National

12. Edinburgh Castle overlooking Princes Street, the main thoroughfare of Scotland's capital city. You can also see the pinnacle of the Scott Monument, and behind it the Scottish Royal Academy and National Gallery

Museum of Antiquities, in Queen Street, is a treasure-house of archaeology. It has some fine Celtic jewelry, early silver dug up from the Celtic fort on Traprain Law, and a room full of finds from Newstead Roman Fort (Trimontium). If you walk past the cases of stone axes and arrow-heads you will find a full-scale model of a British war chariot. It was made for a television documentary.

The same building houses the National Portrait Gallery of Scotland.

The Royal Scottish Museum in Chambers Street is famous for its engineering models. (They work.) It has a magnificent new natural history wing, illustrating the evolution of life. The older galleries have hundreds of stuffed animals and birds, including an example of the extinct dodo. This museum is very popular on Sunday afternoons – a time you should avoid, if you are seriously interested and not just sheltering from the rain!

Edinburgh's own history is illustrated in Huntly House Museum, in the Canongate. (This is the lower half of the Royal Mile.) Across the road is the Canongate Tolbooth, which carries changing historical exhibitions. Further up, John Knox's House (so-called) is a very good example of early burgh building, and Lady Stair's House has relics of the writers Scott, Burns and Stevenson. In the Royal Mile you will also find the fascinating Museum of Childhood, with a collection of toys, books, games and dolls going back four thousand years, although most of them are Victorian or Edwardian. The Wax Museum is a smaller version of Madame Tussaud's. Of course it concentrates on famous Scottish figures. (Yes, there is a Chamber of Horrors.)

Charlotte Square behind the west end of Princes Street is considered to be the finest piece of Georgian architecture in Edinburgh. It was designed by Robert Adam, although alterations were made to his plan. At Number 7 in the north side the National Trust for Scotland has opened the Georgian House. This has been superbly re-furnished in the original New Town style. The drawing-room has several figures dressed in contemporary costume. In the kitchen downstairs you will see rows of copper pans, sugar and salt-choppers, roasting-spits, etc. – all the equipment of the pre-gas and pre-electricity kitchen. In a small side room there is a continuous slide-show on the history of the New Town.

Edinburgh is full of art galleries. The two buildings that face Princes Street at the foot of the Mound are the Royal Scottish Academy and the National Gallery. They look like over-decorated Greek temples. There is a Gallery of Modern Art at Inverleith House, in the beautiful setting of the Botanic Gardens.

There are several smaller museums outside Edinburgh. Here are a few of them. Myreton Motor Museum, at Aberlady in East Lothian, has a collection of vintage cars. In Duns,

13. Kitchen in the Georgian House, Charlotte Square, Edinburgh. The whole house re-creates the life of a wealthy Edinburgh family in the early 1800s

Berwickshire, there is a Jim Clark Room displaying the trophies won by the World Champion. At Livingston, West Lothian, and at East Linton, East Lothian, there are eighteenth-century grain mills. They are water-powered and have been brought back to working order.

Do not miss the Fisheries Museum at Anstruther, Fife. It is at the harbour, in an old building that has been connected with Fife fishing right back to 1318. It has models of fishing boats, an aquarium, old photographs and whalers' log-books, the mock-up of a ship's bridge, the reconstructed interior of a fisher's cottage – and many, many other items. A few yards away the lightship *North Carr* has been moored at the quayside. This is a floating museum that tells the story of lighthouses and navigation lights in north-east Fife.

Inland at Ceres there is a small but very interesting Fife Folk Museum. The Scottish Museum of Wool Textiles is at Walkerburn, Peeblesshire, in an old mill. It illustrates the history of spinning and weaving in the Borders.

If you like looking at old buildings you will find an overwhelming number in this part of Scotland. The chief abbeys have already been described, and there are many others that have left a few traces. Two survive more completely. At Dunfermline Abbey in Fife the twelfth-century nave is in the round-arched style known as 'Romanesque'. It is a rebuilding of the church founded by Queen Margaret. Robert the Bruce is also buried there.

Inchcolm Priory is on an island in the Forth, and you can reach it by boat from Aberdour. The first church was dedicated to St. Columba, who is supposed to have lived there while preaching to the Picts in eastern Scotland. All the early buildings – except a 'hermit's cell' – were destroyed during raids from Norway. What you see now is the twelfth-century priory founded for Augustinian canons by King Alexander

III. For obvious reasons, islands were favourite places for religious houses. There are traces of a Benedictine priory on another Forth island, the Isle of May.

Scotland is not as rich as England in small parish churches, especially in the country. When it was divided into parishes in the mid-twelfth century, the local barons (who might be abbots or bishops) were supposed to provide each parish with its church. Country parishes tended to come under the control of the great religious houses. Often they did not want to spend money providing a separate place of worship – or at least, not enough money to put up a strong stone building that would last. So early country churches are rare in Scotland. In the burghs, townsfolk went ahead and provided their own. There is a fine set of them in the fishing-villages of south-eastern Fife. There, the tower and steeple were vital landmarks for homing ships.

In the later Middle Ages, rich people, instead of giving money to abbeys and priories, often founded 'collegiate' churches; that is, a place where canons and chaplains would say daily mass for the souls of the founder and his or her family. Sometimes what appears to be a parish church was a collegiate or even abbey or priory church that has changed its function.

Here are a few of the smaller churches you may enjoy looking at. Of course the insides have been adapted for the form of worship used by the Church of Scotland. This usually does not make use of an altar.

Berwickshire: the ruined parish church of Edrom has a very beautiful Norman doorway. It is worth turning aside to look at if you are in the area. Ladykirk, built entirely of stone, is still complete. It is supposed to have been built by James IV in 1500 as a thanks-offering when he escaped drowning in the Tweed. Polwarth is a good example of an eighteenth-century Presbyterian church.

Fife: at Leuchars you can see the fine Norman chancel and

apse of the church built by Robert de Quincey, the owner of the nearby motte-and-bailey castle. At Aberdour there is the ruined church of St. Bridget (thirteenth century); and at St. Monance the beautifully restored fourteenth-century church seems to grow out of the volcanic rocks on which it sits, a few yards from the sea. Look out for the full-rigged model of a sailing ship, date about 1800, that hangs from the ceiling.

The Lothians have some very fine early churches. In East Lothian Gifford has Yester Kirk, a charming eighteenth-century building that matches the Improvers' village. St. Mary's in Haddington was known as the 'Lamp of Lothian' and was built on a magnificent scale, two hundred feet in length. The nave is used as the parish church. John Knox attended it as a boy, and buried there is Jane Welsh, who married Thomas Carlyle. Pencaitland is a jumble from the thirteenth to the seventeenth centuries, but it has some quaint details. Whitekirk has a massive tower with a wooden spire. There is a two-storeyed tithe-barn standing nearby – very rare in Scotland. Like so many Scottish churches, it was deliberately set on fire, but not by the English. It was badly damaged by Suffragettes in 1914.

There are two important collegiate churches in East Lothian: one at Dunglass, built by Sir Alexander Hume in 1450; the other at Seton (late fourteenth century). There are tomb effigies of the Setons inside. Both these churches like others of the same type have heavy stone roof slabs.

Another stone-roofed collegiate church was built by a Forrester in 1429 when he was Lord Chamberlain of Scotland. This is the parish church of Corstorphine, a western suburb of Edinburgh. High on the outside of the east gable is a modern electric version of the lamp that shone every night to guide travellers over the dangerous marshes between Edinburgh and Corstorphine.

If you are in the city 'church-hunting' there is the strange

14. Rosslyn Chapel: begun in 1446 as a burial place for the Sinclairs, but only the elaborately-carved choir was finished. The famous 'Apprentice Pillar' is on the right.

Triduana's Chapel attached to Restalrig Church (fifteenth century).

In West Lothian there are two churches which still have a lot of twelfth-century detail: Kirkliston and Dalmeny. At Torphichen is the Preceptory of the Knights of St. John. With its high grim walls it looks more like a castle than a church, and that is perhaps fitting for the Knights Hospitallers.

The tower of Linlithgow parish church, St. Michael's, used to have the same kind of open-work crown as St. Giles in Edinburgh. It now carries a modern structure representing Christ's Crown of Thorns.

Most of the churches mentioned may look rather bare and plain compared with English churches. However, at Roslin in Midlothian, the elaborate workmanship is overpowering. It is the finest of the collegiate churches; like so many, it was never finished. (The choir and chancel for the divine offices were thought more important than the nave, where the congregation, if any, would worship. Often the money would run out before the nave was reached.)

Inside and out, Rosslyn Chapel is a perfect example of the sermon in stone. The carvings run riot over every surface. There are parables, Old and New Testament figures, birds, beasts and foliage swarming everywhere. The most elaborate of all is the famous 'Apprentice Pillar'. This is supposed to have been carved by an apprentice while his master was away. On returning the master killed him in a fit of jealousy at the beautiful work he could not match. It must have been a very long absence, to give time for such detailed carving. In any case, the story is a little suspect – it is also found in the Greek myth of Daedalus.

Until well into the 1600s all dwellings in Scotland were built mostly for protection. The builders had no time to think of display or pleasure. There are hundreds of these fortified houses in the Lowlands. They range from small private towers to huge castles kept by the royal constables. A small number will be described here.

The oldest 'castle' in the Lowlands is probably Edinshill Broch. This is near Abbey St. Bathans in Berwickshire. Brochs were round towers with galleries in the thickness of their walls. They were built by Iron Age people from the first century B.C. to the first century A.D. They are found only in Scotland, and are mostly in the extreme north-east, and in the Western Isles. It is most unusual to find one so far south.

The earliest real castles were built by the Norman overlords of Scotland. They were of the motte-and-bailey type seen in the Bayeux tapestry. The bailey was a piece of ground surrounded by a ditch and bank. Inside it was the motte, a mound of earth. On top of the mound was a wooden tower, surrounded by a fence or palisade. Obviously only the mounds now survive.

The owners of the motte-and-bailey castles probably began to build in stone soon after they arrived. There was certainly plenty of it. But most of our larger castles date from the thirteenth century. They are 'castles of enclosure', a set of towers joined by a wall. This had to be thick enough to stand up to rams and catapults – siege engines that now came into use again. (The Hellenistic Greeks and the Romans had used them first.)

The owner now lived not in the middle keep, but in one of the towers on the wall, known as the *donjon*. It was usually larger than the others and away from the entrance to the castle. You can see this at Dirleton Castle, East Lothian, although later building has altered it a little.

Later the idea of passive defence turned into something more aggressive. The gatehouse or entrance now became the main point of defence. Doune Castle in Perthshire is the best known example of this type of castle. In our area you can see

15. Tantallon Castle, 'impregnable in war' (Scott), towers above the North Sea. It belonged to the powerful Douglas family

one at Tantallon, a stronghold of the Douglases. It stands on steep cliffs above the North Sea, looking out to the Bass Rock, and it is one of the grandest ruins in Scotland.

There are other romantically-placed castles. Castle Campbell perches on the side of the Ochils above the town of Dollar. It is well worth the climb, if only for the striking view across the Forth valley. The place was first known as Castle Gloom; on either side down the glen ran the Burn of Sorrow and the Burn of Care. The name Dollar is said to come from *doulour*, which was Norman-French for 'sadness'.

By taking a ferry from Kinross you can visit the island castle of Loch Leven where Queen Mary was imprisoned for a year in 1567. There are other castles associated with her in our area. Craigmillar, on the outskirts of Edinburgh, is where she retired for a time after the murder of her Italian secretary, David Riccio. Hermitage is set in the wild moorland of Liddesdale. It passed from the Douglases to the Earl of Bothwell, who was the Keeper of Liddesdale. Mary visited him here after he was wounded in a Border fight. She rode fifty miles on a stormy autumn day. Scandalmongers made a great deal of this.

Crichton in Midlothian is another fine castle that belonged to the Earl of Bothwell.

Strictly speaking these last four are not castles. They are large examples of the Scottish tower house.

The tower house was simply what its name suggests. Often it had a door above ground level which had to be reached by a ladder. This was a primitive form of drawbridge. Later houses were often surrounded by or joined to a wall enclosing other buildings. The enclosure was known as a *barmkin*. The tower house with its barmkin often looks like a castle of enclosure, especially if it is on a large scale.

In the tower house one room sat on top of another, rather than beside it. People went from room to room by using the *turnpike* or spiral stair. This was built in the angle of two walls and very narrow – which made it easy to defend, if anyone tried to enter the house unlawfully. The 'pepper-pot' turrets of old Scots houses are often concealed stairways.

This tall, vertical building gave great protection to the people living in it; it impressed the neighbours (the owner was often responsible for law and order in his own area); and even when life was more peaceful it made the least possible use of timber. The ceiling of one room formed the floor of the one above it. There was little home-grown timber until the end of the eighteenth century. A lot was imported, but that made it more expensive.

However, a kind of compromise was made between this economy and the nuisance of always having to use a stairway to reach another room. The simple square tower evolved into the L-plan, the T-plan and the Z-plan house. These gave at least a few rooms side by side; and when hand-guns became smaller and more accurate, they also provided more angles of fire to pick off attackers.

These tower houses, dating from the fourteenth to the seventeenth century, can be seen all over the Lowlands. Many of them are still occupied. The finest of all is considered to be Borthwick Castle in Midlothian.

In the Borders, tower houses are called *peels*, or *peel towers*. (Peel really means the timber palisade surrounding a tower, but the name is traditional, though incorrect.) During the fifteenth and sixteenth centuries, the time of the Border raids and reivers, a great many peels were built. A 1535 Act of Parliament urged all £100 landowners to provide themselves with a barmkin and tower 'in trublous tyme'. Some were built as temporary places of refuge, or as watch-towers fitted with warning-bell and beacon. When Scott stayed on his grandfather's farm as a boy his imagination was fired by the nearby Smailholm Tower. Newark Castle on the Yarrow near Selkirk, and Neidpath Castle on the Tweed near Peebles are larger examples of the peel tower.

All the tower houses named are open to the public. You will notice dozens of others as you travel around. Nigel Tranter's *The Fortified House in Scotland* describes and illustrates every known example.

Near the tower houses in farming country you will often see

strange little buildings, also in stone. They look like tall thin bee-hives, or they are square-shaped, with slate roofs sloping one way. These are the earlier and later forms of the *doo-cot* (pigeon loft). Up till the nineteenth century they were vital for providing fresh meat in winter, although the birds were great destroyers of the crops. There is a fine example outside Dirleton Castle, and another at Phantassie, near East Linton.

Not all old houses in the Lowlands are castles and places of defence. At Linlithgow and Falkland there are two great courtyard palaces, with some of the earliest Renaissance architecture in Britain.

Falkland was a royal hunting-lodge. Tilting, archery, tennis, hawking, and chasing boars and deer in the Forest of Falkland were favourite pastimes of the Stuart kings and queens. The forest was carefully preserved. When James IV built the *Great Michael* in 1512, the biggest ship in Europe, he 'waistit all the wodis in Fyfe except Falkland wode'. After the Stuarts even Falkland Forest disappeared.

There are traces of an earlier castle in the palace garden. In it the young Duke of Rothesay, heir to the kingdom, was supposed to have been starved to death by his uncle, the Duke of Albany. Sir Walter Scott wrote about it in *The Fair Maid of Perth*. Much of the Renaissance palace has gone, and its site has been turned into a beautiful garden by the National Trust for Scotland. The magnificent south range is still intact. This was built in 1539 for James V and his French queen, Mary of Lorraine. The architect was the King's cousin, Sir James Hamilton, who had spent a long time in France, and the master masons were French. The whole building is a fine monument to the Auld Alliance between Scotland and France. In the garden there is a 'real tennis' court, similar to the one in Hampton Court Palace on the Thames.

Mary Queen of Scots, daughter of James V and Mary of

16. Linlithgow Palace, birthplace of Mary, Queen of Scots. In the background is the modern 'Crown of Thorns' on St. Michael's Church

Lorraine, was born at Linlithgow Palace. Like Falkland, it stood on the site of an earlier castle. The palace overlooked Linlithgow Loch and was built gradually between 1424 and 1540. It caught fire when occupied by the Duke of Cumberland's soldiers in 1746, and is now only a magnificent shell. Bonnie Prince Charlie had been entertained there the year before. In early days, the water level of the loch may have been forty feet higher than it is now, so the Palace mound would have been an island. Mary of Lorraine when taken there said she 'had never seen a more princely palace'. In the inner courtyard are the remains of an elaborately carved fountain, and there is a gigantic fireplace in the main hall.

There are some beautiful country houses in the eastern Lowlands, but only a few can be mentioned. The oldest is Traquair House at Innerleithen near Peebles. It is supposed to date from the tenth century, which would make it the oldest inhabited house in Scotland. Over the ten centuries it has passed to many different families and been greatly altered. Despite this it has a very satisfying, unified look about it.

The Earls of Traquair were ardent Jacobites. The famous Bear Gates, the main entrance to the grounds, are never opened. One story says the fifth earl shut them after promising Bonnie Prince Charlie that they would never be opened until a Stuart came back to the throne.

Traquair was an important strong-point in the Wars of Independence. It then stood on a bend of the Tweed, but this was diverted to protect the foundations of the house.

Besides being a fascinating building, Traquair is full of historical relics. In the Museum Room are family portraits and letters, Jacobite glass, and a rosary, crucifix and purse that belonged to Queen Mary. There is also an eighteenth-century brewhouse in full working order.

Another famous country house is The Binns, the home of General Tam Dalyell, who raised the Royal Scots Greys for Charles II. Despite later alterations it is basically a seventeenth-century building. This is very early for an unfortified country house in Scotland.

In the eighteenth century scores of fine houses in the classical or Georgian style were built in the Scottish countryside. Some are now hotels or schools; most are still privately owned. They can be seen from the outside on days when their gardens are opened to the public. A few of the houses are open too, and fortunately they include the two most important Adam houses in southern Scotland.

William Adam was a Scottish architect (1689–1748) who built about twenty country mansions for Scottish landowners, as well as carrying out important work for the Government. His three sons, John, James and Robert, continued his work – literally, for in some cases they altered or completed their father's buildings. Robert Adam is the most famous (1728–1792), and the 'Adam Style' of interior decoration is as well known in England as it is in Scotland.

Mellerstain is nine miles north-east of Melrose. From the outside it is an imposing Georgian mansion, although there is a parapet round the roof in the later 'Gothic' style. There is a charming garden falling down to the lake, and splendid views of the Cheviots, but it is the interior that visitors come for. This is all in the 'Adam style' of delicate colours, and interior fittings such as carpets and fireplaces and door-handles designed by Robert Adam to blend together. There is superb plasterwork on the ceilings and wall-friezes.

Mellerstain is closely connected with Lady Grisel Baillie, though she knew only the two side wings built by William Adam. It was her grandson who commissioned Robert Adam to add to his father's work on the house.

Lady Grisel was the daughter of Sir Patrick Hume, later first Earl of Marchmont. Her own family and that of the Baillies (into which she later married) were staunch Covenanters. Both families were in great danger in the 1680s, and finally they all fled to Holland, until the coming of William of Orange. Before this Lady Grisel's father was forced to hide for a month in the vaults of the church at Polwarth, a mile from their home. She 'went every night by herself, at midnight, to carry him victuals and drink, and staid with him as long as she could'. (This is Lady Grisel's daughter writing.) It was difficult for the young girl to get food without the servants suspecting. 'The only way it was done was, by stealing it off her plate at dinner into her lap . . . Her father liked sheep's head; and while the children were eating their broth, she had conveyed most of one into her lap; when her brother Sandy

... had done, he looked up with astonishment, and said, "Mother, will ye look at Grisel; while we have been eating our broth, she has eat up the whole sheep's head".'

It is pleasant to know that the story of the two families had a happy ending. There are several portraits of Lady Grisel in Mellerstain.

17. Hopetoun House, on the shores of the Forth near Queensferry. This is Scotland's greatest Adam mansion

The most famous Adam building in Scotland is Hopetoun House, on the south shore of the Forth, near the two Bridges. It is also the biggest and the most impressive. It was remodelled from an earlier house built by Sir William Bruce, the man who modernised Holyrood Palace. Hopetoun House consists of a huge central building in classical style, with projecting wings at each end. From the wings curving porticoes sweep out to smaller buildings or 'pavilions'. William Adam, and his two sons John and Robert, all had a hand in this design. The approach road running between vast lawns makes the most of the house's overpowering façade.

Hopetoun is surrounded by lovely woods with deer and other wild animals. There is a Preservation Trust which helps maintain the interior fittings – furniture, library books and so on. It also has a Museum of the Horse, and an Education Day Centre which in all sorts of ways tries to involve visitors actively in the upkeep of one of the great treasures of Scottish culture.

Bowhill, near Selkirk, is a nineteenth-century house that is visited mainly for its paintings and works of art. Of these later houses the most famous is Abbotsford, the home of Sir Walter Scott. When he bought it in 1812 the site was a one-hundred-and-ten-acre farm on the right bank of the Tweed. It had all the romantic associations that he loved. The land had once belonged to the monks of Melrose, and it was surrounded by ancient, historic places.

At that time Scott was a famous poet. He had written *The Lay of the Last Minstrel, The Lady of the Lake* and *Marmion* and other long poems. He yearned to be a landowner, and when he began the Waverley novels in 1815 he soon had enough money to pull down the old farmhouse and begin a much grander building. He also bought up more and more land around it. Abbotsford was ready to move into in 1824. By that time Scott's debts had piled up, and he had ruined his health with over-work. He had only eight years in which to enjoy being the owner of Abbotsford.

The house is more of a literary shrine than a country house. The rooms are full of souvenirs and curios, for Scott was an avid collector. You will enjoy looking at the weapons and armour. There are also items such as Flora Macdonald's pocket book, Rob Roy's purse, dirk and broadsword, some relics from the battlefield of Waterloo, a lock of Prince Charlie's hair – the list is endless. There are personal mementoes of Scott himself as well.

The outside of the house is a strange mixture. It is partly 'Scots baronial' (pepper-pot turrets and crow-stepped gables), blended with the wide-headed windows and oriels found in country houses in the English Cotswolds.

Scott the collector appears even here. High up on the wall to the left of the main porch is the door from the condemned cell of the old Tolbooth in Edinburgh, which was pulled down in 1817. There is a reason for the strange position of the door. In the Tolbooth, it led outside to a flat roof on which stood the gallows – a grisly arrangement that Scott copied. (Not the gallows, of course!)

7 · Out and About

If you are coming to the eastern Lowlands for an outdoor holiday, it is very likely that you will be staying somewhere close to the sea. Depending on their size, the seaside towns offer all the usual holiday amusements – bathing, fun-fairs, beach-rides, and so on. You cannot expect so many sun-baked days as you might in southern England. You will enjoy yourself much more if you come prepared for activities such as sailing, fishing, walking or water-skiing.

The Berwickshire coastline is as grand as anything you will find in the Western Highlands. There are impressive stretches of towering cliffs all the way from Eyemouth to Dunbar in East Lothian. At St. Abbs Head they rise to three hundred feet. There is more fine cliff-scenery in south-east Fife.

These rugged cliffs are a paradise for geologists and bird-watchers. Geological and nature trails have been set up at Barns Ness near Dunbar, and at Yellowcraig two miles west of North Berwick. For really keen bird-watchers there is Tentsmuir Point in Fife and Aberlady Bay in East Lothian. Both these places are Nature Reserves. They are well known for their wildfowl and waders, which are best studied in winter. On the Forth islands there are colonies of eiders, terns, auks, kittiwakes and cormorants. If you book a visit with the Nature Conservancy Council you can catch a boat at Crail and go to the Field Station on the Isle of May. The officers there study bird migration.

The most famous bird sanctuary in the area is the Bass

18. The Bass Rock: a party of sight-seers on their way from North Berwick to view the steep cliffs and huge gannet colonies

Rock, which is a breeding ground for about eighteen thousand gannets. You can take a day-trip from North Berwick. Like the nearby Berwick Law, the Bass is a volcanic plug. Its shape is unmistakable, and the sheer sides are white with the droppings of the huge bird colonies. The Bass itself has a romantic history. It has been used as a strong-point to control shipping, and as a prison. When William of Orange came to the British throne, four young Jacobites seized the Rock and held out for three years. They plundered passing ships for their supplies.

The Loch Leven Nature Centre was the first to be set up in Britain. It is housed in a converted farm-building at the side of the loch. The loch is Britain's most important stretch of fresh water for wildfowl, mostly geese and duck.

A fairly new development in southern Scotland are the country parks. In West Lothian there are the Almondell and Calderwood Country Park (two hundred and twenty acres)

and the much larger 650-acre Beecraigs in the Bathgate Hills. These parks offer picnic and barbecue sites, walks and nature trails, and of course a vast amount of wild plant and animal life. You can wander round on your own or join guided walks with enticing names like 'Fruits and Nuts', 'Adam's Ale', 'Midsummer Potions'.

The Forestry Commission does a lot to provide activities for tourists. You can walk about at random, or follow nature trails, at Craik Forest near Hawick, and the Glentress Forest near Peebles. The enormous Borders Forest Park spreads north across the Border. You can enter the Scottish section at Wauchope near Bonchester Bridge or at Newcastleton. Both these are in Roxburghshire.

Following the same trend many country houses have now laid out trails in their parkland. You will find some in the grounds of Duns Castle, Hopetoun House and Dalkeith House. Other stately homes open their private gardens to visitors during the summer months. A booklet published every year, *Scotland's Gardens Scheme*, gives full details. It is on sale at most large newsagents in Scotland.

Even if your holiday is based in a town you can make an interesting walk by following a 'heritage trail'. This is a suggested route that will take you round the most interesting sights in the town. You can obtain a pamphlet on this at the local tourist office in North Berwick, Linlithgow, Haddington, St. Monance and Dunbar.

Remember too that most Scottish cities have open country on their doorsteps, or even inside their boundaries. Edinburgh's Holyrood Park and Blackford Hill will give you some very hilly scrambles. Edinburgh also has the Water of Leith and Cramond Walkways. You can follow them with free leaflets issued by the Tourist Information Offices. Slightly outside the town there is the Union Canal Walk. You can start out in the heart of the city, but unless you are set on covering every inch the first built-up sections are not very interesting. Slightly more unusual is the five-and-a-half-mile Railway Walk along the disused track between Pencaitland and Ormiston, in East Lothian.

Obviously, the Lowlands do not provide the really wild scenery you find in the Highlands; but there is plenty of quite rough upland walking. In Fife, you can explore the Lomonds above Loch Leven. You can climb the East Lomond (one thousand four hundred and seventy-one feet) by starting from a village called Scotlandwell. The Lothians have the Bathgate Hills, the Lammermuirs and the Pentlands. These hills are criss-crossed by dozens of hills and tracks, some of them the old droving roads. In the Borders, you can follow the old routes across the Cheviots, or the Eildons, or go further west into the wild moorland between Peebles and St. Mary's Loch. There are several hill-paths marked round here. At Kirk Yetholm you can begin to walk down the Pennine Way, and part of ancient Dere Street has now been marked out: from St. Boswells down to Jedfoot, Kale Water and Cocquet. If you like, you can follow it over the Border to High Rochester in Northumberland.

Before you begin any kind of hill-walking remember that what appears to be open country is probably someone's sheep-walk, shooting-moor, or even an army weapon-testing range. At certain times there may be restrictions on walking in this area, and it would be sensible to find out what they are. People who live locally can be helpful about this. If you want to enquire beforehand, the Scottish Ramblers' Association and the Scottish Rights of Way Society can give you advice about hill-paths and routes over open moorland.

Walking in the hills can often be combined with your own archaeological trail. Scattered about the Lowlands there are about eighty standing stones, either alone or in small groups. They were put up some time between 2000 B.C. and 1000 B.C., perhaps as boundary-marks, perhaps to point out routes or meeting-places. It has been suggested recently that they were for studying the cycles of the moon and stars. That would make them a primitive form of calendar. Some of them are found with burial cairns of a later date.

The most striking site is at Cairnpapple Hill in West Lothian, near Torphichen. It has a small museum as well. There is a stone circle and ditch, with a Bronze Age cairn burial. The whole site was probably used for worship and burial from about 2000 B.C. to 400 B.C.

Carvings called 'cup and ring marks' are found on some of these stones. No one is sure what they meant. Possibly they were for some religious purpose. The caves north-east of West Wemyss in Fife have a lot of these strange carvings, mixed with others that are early Christian in date.

A later kind of prehistoric monument is the Iron Age fort. Between 600 B.C. and A.D. 100 many examples were put up in south-east Scotland. There is a great cluster of them in Upper Tweeddale, near Peebles. There are nearly as many on the hills overlooking the Leader Water, and some on the Pentlands and upper Ettrick Water. A few of them have been found on the steep hill slopes of Fife and Kinross-shire.

These forts were usually on hill-tops or ridges. They were defended by walls made of earth or stone, sometimes 'laced' with timber posts to strengthen them. The walls enclosed an area of upwards of one acre, and there would have been a huddle of small huts inside them. It has been suggested that they were built during fighting between the three major tribes of southern Scotland, the Selgovae of the upper Tweed, the Votadini of Lothian and Berwickshire, and the Venicones of Fife.

Unless you have a trained eye you will usually see only a muddle of humps and banks under the turf. But a few forts are more obvious. At the Chesters, near Haddington, you can make out the ramparts quite easily. At Castle Law (Glencorse, near Edinburgh) there is an underground stone gallery, known as a *souterrain*. Eildon Hill North and Traprain Law both had large forts about forty acres in size. After storming the North Eildon Agricola's soldiers built the Roman fort of Newstead, 'Trimontium'.

Apart from Dere Street, you will not find many striking Roman remains in this area. In Midlothian there is a Roman fortlet at Castle Greg, near West Calder, and a fort at Lyne, four miles west of Peebles; at Woden Law overlooking the Kale Water there are some Roman siege-works. These were built for practice round an abandoned fort. There is a very well-preserved section of Dere Street nearby. At Cramond, outside Edinburgh, you can see the foundations of the Severan fort (early third century A.D.) picked out in the churchyard. A little below in a carpark some more buildings are being excavated.

The Antonine Wall begins within West Lothian. The only visible sign of it in this area is a copy of a distance slab that marked the end of a section of the Wall. The original is in the National Museum of Antiquities in Edinburgh. The copy has been set into a wall near Bridgeness Tower. It shows a Roman cavalryman riding down four barbarians.

Another way of taking an out-of-doors holiday is to link it with some sport or activity that interests you. The British Council for Archaeology publishes a list of 'digs' where volunteers are wanted. Enterprise Youth and the National Conservation Corps (Scotland) organise holiday projects at work-camps throughout Scotland. (You do however have to be over sixteen to join these two.)

The Borders Regional Council runs Outdoor Education Residential Centres at Grantshouse, Pyatshaw, Scotch Kershope and Towford. These of course are group activities, and priority is given to local schools and organisations. Enquiries are however invited from other bodies, and there is a pamphlet giving details.

Youth Hostelling has been popular for many years. Outside Edinburgh there are nine Youth Hostels in south-east Scotland, all close to good walking and cycling country. Some of them also organize special activities. At Snoot, near Hawick, and at Melrose, the Y.H.A. arranges pony-trekking holidays. The Borders are Scotland's horse country. There are dozens of riding-schools here, and nearly as many in Fife and the Lothians. The schools can arrange pony-treks for you into the nearby hills; if you are an experienced rider they will hire out ponies daily. Otherwise you have to be accompanied. Some schools are willing to take out children of all ages down to four!

All round the east coast there are Sailing-Clubs. There is inland sailing too, at St. Mary's Loch. At Aberdour and North Queensferry there are sailing-schools for the absolute beginner. In Fife at Lochgelly, there is Water-Skiing. You can also go sub-aqua diving on the Berwickshire coast at Coldingham, and be taught to fly-fish at Peebles and Walkerburn. There are salmon in the three T's: Tay, Tweed and Teviot, and the sport there is world-famous. There are plenty of brown trout and rainbow trout in the streams and reservoirs, and sea trout are found nearer the coast.

Sea-angling is free; but fresh-water fishing, especially in the prized Border streams and rivers, is usually protected and expensive. Daily charges, however, are sometimes quite reasonable. It is best to ask locally about permits and charges. You can do this at angling-clubs, or any shop that sells fishing-tackle. Lothian Region issues a helpful little booklet on fresh-water fishing in its own area.

You can now ski in summer, in Scotland. The artificial slope on the Pentlands, at Hillend, is used all year round. The chairlift can be used by walkers as well. There is a smaller artificial slope at Jedburgh.

Golf is thought of as a sport for the middle-aged; in Scotland, perhaps more than in England, it is a young person's sport as well. Fife has about thirty courses, the Lothians forty-four (including the twelve on dunes near the sea), and there are twenty more in the Borders.

More unusual sports are becoming popular in this area. There is gliding at Portmoak, off the steep western side of Bishop Hill in Kinross-shire. There are enthusiastic supporters for the newer sports of hang-gliding, orienteering, and parachuting. Details of all these can be found in a free booklet issued by the Scottish Sports Council.

All these sports have their own competitions and tournaments. Many of them take place during the summer, when they help to amuse holiday-makers. At this time many places also put on cycle races, sand-yachting and vintage car displays.

One sport you will not see if you are only a summer visitor is the Border Rugby 'Sevens'. These famous matches are played off in April at Melrose, Hawick and Jedburgh, and at Kelso in September. Most Borderers are fanatically interested in rugby, and many famous players have come from this part of Scotland.

Jedburgh has its 'Candlemas Handba' in February. Uppies play Downies all over the town in a primitive football match. Team numbers are unlimited. Shopkeepers usually barricade their windows while the game is on. Handba is supposed to go back to an ancient Border skirmish, when the Scots played football with the heads of the English they had slain.

The larger towns provide all the usual spectator sports the whole year round. Edinburgh has also the Royal Commonwealth Pool and the Meadowbank Sports Centre, built for the 1970 Commonwealth Games.

If you are visiting any of the Borders towns in June or July you will be drawn into the festivities linked with the Common Riding. This began with the ancient ceremony in which officials used to mark out the land belonging to the burgh. In some places the Common Riding is a genuine survival from very early days; in others, it is an old custom that has been revived. But in all the towns the original Riding has now turned into a summer festival with sports, athletics, processions, dancing, and other celebrations. Visitors flock from miles around, and ex-Borderers make special journeys to be present.

The main feature is still a mounted procession. In Hawick it turns into a gallop, when the Cornet holding up his standard leads a chase up the hill to St. Leonard's. At Galashiels there is the Braw Lad's Gathering, led by the Lad and the Braw Lass. At Jedburgh there is the Redeswire Ride. At Selkirk the centre of the whole event is the 'Casting of the Colours'. This recalls the death of Selkirk men who went to the Battle of Flodden in 1514. As the flag is dipped in front of the statue of a mounted Border reiver, a band plays the haunting lament 'The Flouers o' the Forest' – a moving link between ancient and recent disasters, for the statue is Selkirk's memorial to the dead of two World Wars.

The Border towns are also busy agricultural centres, with regular sales of livestock. Hawick's claims to be the oldest in Britain. Then there are regular Agricultural Shows, Flower Shows, Kelso's Ram Sales, and the Border Shepherds' Show. If you are lucky you will find sheepdog trials at other times and places as well.

The biggest agricultural event in Scotland is the Royal Highland Show, held at Ingliston outside Edinburgh, in early June. All aspects of country life, not just farming, are represented in this big event. While it is on it occupies more space than anything else in local newspapers. It may seem

19. Galashiels: the traditional Common Ridings are the centre of summer festivities in the Border towns. Here the Braw Lad and Braw Lass lead the 'Gathering'

strange to have the show at Edinburgh: it is held there because it was so expensive to have a Highland Show rotating round the various places that competed for the honour of holding it. In 1960 it was given a permanent home – very far south of the Highland Line!

The list of fairs, festivals, parades and pageants held in south-east Scotland grows longer every year, and there are a great many that have not been mentioned. The seaside towns have their own variation. There is the Seafood Festival at Anstruther, and Herring Queen Week at Eyemouth. The armed forces stationed in Scotland have their own occasions. There are open Navy Days at Rosyth Naval Base, on the north side of the Forth, and Open Days at Leuchars Royal Air Force Base.

Go to any local Information or Tourist Office. The staff will be happy to give you leaflets on every possible kind of activity and amusement that can help you to enjoy your holiday. You will probably leave thinking that the eastern Lowlands need their long, cold winter to sit back and recover from all these exhausting pursuits!

8 · More Information

The Ordnance Survey maps for the eastern Lowlands are Numbers 58, 59, 65, 66, 67, 73, 74, 75 (Revised Metric Edition). They replace the earlier one-inch series and are more up-to-date than earlier maps. These of course are on a large scale of 1 : 50,000.

Many can be obtained at most large bookshops or from the H.M.S.O. bookshop in Castle Street, Edinburgh. This is near Princes Street. There you can also buy detailed guides to all the buildings looked after by the Ministry of Works, or Department of the Environment as it now is. You can of course buy the guides at the sites. At the H.M.S.O. bookshop you can buy *Scotland's Countryside* – the most useful short list of important gardens, nature reserves, and historic buildings in each area of Scotland. Also available is Volume VI in the series *Illustrated Guide to Ancient Monuments*, *Scottish Castles* and *Scottish Abbeys*. These books are not so attractively produced as the more modern coloured brochures you can find in any bookshop, but they cover the ground more thoroughly and their information is accurate.

If you find these volumes rather daunting the Scottish Tourist Board has pamphlets and maps for tourists covering specialised interests (e.g., golf, angling, hill-walking, etc.). The main office is on Waverley Bridge, just outside Waverley Station in Edinburgh. The STB generously gives away dozens of well-illustrated leaflets in colour. They contain small-scale maps with bold symbols that show at a glance what each area holds. The Board's larger publications are sold at a very reasonable price. The STB has links with Tourist and Information Offices in all the Scottish towns, and from them you can obtain literature on the local area.

Another organisation well worth contacting is the National Trust for Scotland, which maintains various gardens and historic buildings throughout Scotland. At each of these you can buy very attractive guides. The Trust's *Yearbook* gives a complete list of the places it looks after.

Your own local library is sure to have some books on Scotland in its travel section. When you are on holiday do not feel that you cannot make use of the local library because you are a visitor – the staff will be very pleased to help you, and you can read the books in the library, even if you cannot arrange to borrow them. The best guidebooks are often those written for local circulation only. They usually have far more detail than the national guides. If you are able to use it, probably the best collection of guidebooks of all kinds is in the Scottish Library Room of the Central Public Library on George IV Bridge in Edinburgh. There is a section for each of the Scottish counties.

Here now are two lists. The first is of useful addresses, and the second of books where you can read more about the eastern Lowlands of Scotland.

Useful addresses

Borders Regional Council (Tourist Information) Newtown St. Boswells, Roxburghs.

Cyclists' Touring Club National Headquarters, Cotterell House, 69 Meadrow, Godalming, Surrey GU7 3HS.

Department of Recreation and Leisure, Lothian Regional Council, 40 Torpichen Street, Edinburgh 3.

Enterprise Youth, 49 Melville Street, Edinburgh 3.

Fife Regional Council (Tourist Information), Fife House, North Street, Glenrothes, Fife.

Fife Water Ski Club, 220 High Street, Kirkcaldy, Fife.

The Forestry Commission, 231 Corstorphine Road, Edinburgh 12.

The Manager, Hillend Ski Centre, Biggar Road, Edinburgh EH10 7DU.

National Conservation Corps (Scotland), c/o 70 Main Street, Doune, Perthshire.

Nature Conservancy Council, 12 Hope Terrace, Edinburgh EH9 2AS.

Northern Lighthouse Board, 84 George Street, Edinburgh 4.

National Trust for Scotland, 5 Charlotte Square, Edinburgh EH2 4DU.

The Ramblers' Association (Scottish Area), c/o 173 Braidcroft Road, Glasgow G53 0HG.

Royal Society for the Protection of Birds, 17 Regent Terrace, EH7 5BN.

Royal Yachting Association Scottish Council, 8 Frederick Street, Edinburgh EH2 2HB.

Scottish Association of Youth Clubs, 13 Eglinton Crescent, Edinburgh EH3 8HQ.

Scottish Canoe Association, c/o 7 Denoon Terrace, Dundee DD2 2EL.

Scottish Caravan Club, c/o 53 Craigcrook Avenue, Edinburgh EH4 3PU.

Scottish Cyclists' Union, c/o 293 Rosemount Place, Aberdeen, AB2 4YB.

Scotland's Gardens Scheme, 26 Castle Terrace, Edinburgh 1.

Scottish Gliding Union, Portmoak, Scotlandwell, Fife.

Scottish National Camps Association Ltd., 57 Melville Street, Edinburgh 3.

Scottish Orienteering Association, c/o Bernhill, Wester Pitcorthie Road, Dunfermline, Fife, KY11 5DR.

Scottish Ornithologists' Club, 21 Regent Terrace, Edinburgh 7.

Scottish Rights of Way Society, Ltd., 32 Rutland Square, Edinburgh EH1 2BZ.

Scottish Sports Council, 1/3 St. Colme Street, Edinburgh 1.

Scottish Tourist Board, Waverley Bridge, Edinburgh 1.

Scottish Wildlife Trust, 8 Dublin Street, Edinburgh 1.

Scottish Youth Hostels Association, 7 Glebe Crescent, Stirling, FK8 2JA.

Scoutscroft Diving Centre, Coldingham, Berwickshire.

Book list

This is divided into two parts. Part A consists of books written for use in schools; Part B lists books for general reading.

A

CONTEMPORARY SCOTLAND (Heinemann Educational) (1969):
Farming   A. Glen
New Towns   M. Williams
Transport   R. W. McArthur

Edinburgh for Children   Holmes McDougall

SCOTTISH SEARCH SERIES (Holmes McDougall):
Farming and the Countryside 1700–1900   E. Simpson and N. Tate
Industry – Coal and Iron   A. Hogg and M. Maciver
Roads and Canals 1700–1900   I. Donnachie

THEN AND THERE (Longmans):
A Border Town in the Industrial Revolution K. McKechnie (1968)
The Romans in Scotland   O. Thomson (1968)
Edinburgh in its Golden Age   W. K. Ritchie (1967)

B

About St. Andrews and About J. K. Robertson Citizen Office, St. Andrews (1973)

Canals of Scotland J. Lindsay David & Charles (1963)

The Drove Roads of Scotland A. R. B. Haldane David & Charles (1973 ed.)

Edinburgh and South-East Scotland (Regional Archaeologies) G. & A. Ritchie Heinemann Educational (1972)

550 Things to See in Scotland Scottish Tourist Board

The Fortified House in Scotland (Vol. 1: South East Scotland) N. Tranter Oliver & Boyd (1962)

A History of Scotland R. Mitchison Methuen (1970)

The Industrial Archaeology of Scotland (Vol. 1: The Lowlands and Borders) J. Hume Batsford (1976)

The Lowlands I. Finlay Batsford (1967)

The Making of the Scottish Landscape R. N. Millman Batsford (1795)

Old and New Edinburgh Pocket Guide Ramsay Head Press, Edinburgh (1976)

Portrait of the Border Country N. Tranter Robert Hale (1972)

Regional History of the Railways (Vol. 6 Scotland: The Lowlands) J. Thomas David & Charles (1963)

Scotland's Countryside H.M.S.O.

Scottish Hill Tracks (Vol. 1: Southern Scotland) D. G. Moir Bartholomew (1975 ed.)

Scottish Townscape C. McWilliam Collins (1975)

Traditions of Edinburgh R. Chalmers Chambers (various editions)

Who Are the Scots? B.B.C. Pamphlet

Index